SAGE was founded in 1965 by Sara Miller McCune to support the dissemination of usable knowledge by publishing innovative and high-quality research and teaching content. Today, we publish more than 750 journals, including those of more than 300 learned societies, more than 800 new books per year, and a growing range of library products including archives, data, case studies, reports, conference highlights, and video. SAGE remains majority-owned by our founder, and after Sara's lifetime will become owned by a charitable trust that secures our continued independence.

Los Angeles | London | Washington DC | New Delhi | Singapore | Boston

Contemporary Practices of Mahatma Gandhi National Rural Employment Guarantee Scheme

Thank you for choosing a SAGE product! If you have any comment, observation or feedback, I would like to personally hear from you. Please write to me at <u>contactceo@sagepub.in</u>

—Vivek Mehra, Managing Director and CEO,
SAGE Publications India Pvt Ltd, New Delhi

Bulk Sales

SAGE India offers special discounts for purchase of books in bulk. We also make available special imprints and excerpts from our books on demand.

For orders and enquiries, write to us at

Marketing Department
SAGE Publications India Pvt Ltd
B1/I-1, Mohan Cooperative Industrial Area
Mathura Road, Post Bag 7
New Delhi 110044, India
E-mail us at <u>marketing@sagepub.in</u>

Get to know more about SAGE, be invited to SAGE events, get on our mailing list. Write today to <u>marketing@sagepub.in</u>

This book is also available as an e-book.

Contemporary Practices of Mahatma Gandhi National Rural Employment Guarantee Scheme

Insights from Districts

K.B. Saxena

SAGE www.sagepublications.com
Los Angeles • London • New Delhi • Singapore • Washington DC • Boston

First published in 2015 by

 SAGE Publications India Pvt Ltd
B1/I-1 Mohan Cooperative Industrial Area
Mathura Road, New Delhi 110 044, India
www.sagepub.in

SAGE Publications Inc
2455 Teller Road
Thousand Oaks, California 91320, USA

SAGE Publications Ltd
1 Oliver's Yard, 55 City Road
London EC1Y 1SP, United Kingdom

SAGE Publications Asia-Pacific Pte Ltd
3 Church Street
#10-04 Samsung Hub
Singapore 049483

Published by Vivek Mehra for SAGE Publications India Pvt Ltd, typeset at 10/12 pt Minion Pro by Diligent Typesetter, Delhi, and printed at Saurabh Printers Pvt Ltd, New Delhi.

Library of Congress Cataloging-in-Publication Data

Saxena, K. B.
   Contemporary practices of Mahatma Gandhi National Rural Employment Guarantee Scheme : insights from districts / K.B. Saxena.
       pages cm
   Includes index.
   1. National Rural Employment Guarantee Scheme (India). 2. Manpower policy, Rural—India. 3. Guaranteed annual income—India. 4. Rural development—India. I. Title.
       HD5710.85.I4S29   331.12'04240954—dc23   2015   2015003623

ISBN: 978-93-515-0271-5 (PB)

The SAGE Team: N. Unni Nair, Alekha Chandra Jena, Rajib Chatterjee and Ritu Chopra

List of Contributors

Dr K.B. Saxena, IAS (Retd.)
Professor
Social Justice and Governance
Council for Social Development (CSD)
Sangha Rachna
53, Lodi Estate
New Delhi 110003

Dr Ashwini Kumar
Professor
Tata Institute of Social Sciences (TISS)
V.N. Purav Marg, Deonar
Mumbai 400088

Mr M.D. Asthana, IAS (Retd.)
Former Secretary
Department of Statistics
Government of India
New Delhi 110003

Dr K.S. Gopal
Chief Executive Officer
Centre for Environmental Concern
Bharakatpura
Hyderabad 500027

Dr Nilay Ranjan
Consultant (UNDP)
Ministry of Rural Development (MoRD)
Krishi Bhawan
New Delhi 110001

Mr Rajesh Mall
Consultant
Ministry of Rural Development (MoRD)
Krishi Bhawan
New Delhi 110001

Dr H. Hemnath Rao
Professor and Director
Administrative Staff College of India
Bella Vista, Raj Bhavan Road
Hyderabad 500082

Dr Bhagirath Panda
Professor
Department of Economics
North-Eastern Hill University
Shillong, Meghalaya 793022

Dr Pradip Prabhu
Professor
Tata Institute of Social Sciences (TISS)
V.N. Purav Marg, Deonar
Mumbai 400088

Dr V. Suresh Babu
Associate Professor
Centre for Wage Employment and Poverty
Alleviation (CWEPA)
National Institute of Rural Development &
Panchayat Raj (NIRD&PR)
Rajendranagar, Hyderabad 500030

Dr Reetika Khera
Associate Professor
Indian Institute of Technology
Hauz Khas
New Delhi 110016

Contents

List of Abbreviations

AAP	Annual Action Plan
ADC	Area Development Council
ATMA	Agriculture Technology Management Agency
ATTF	All Tripura Tiger Force
BC	Backward Caste
BDO	Block Development Officer
BPM	Block *Panchayat* Member
BPO	Branch Post Office
BRGF	Backward Regions Grant Fund
CEO	Chief Executive Officer
DFO	Divisional Forest Officer
DPC	District Programme Coordinator
DPO	District Programme Officer
DRDA	District Rural Development Agency
EGS	Employment Guarantee Scheme
FRA	Forest Rights Act
FTO	Fund Transfer Order
GDP	Gross Domestic Product
GoI	Government of India
GP	*Gram Panchayat*
GRS	*Gram Rozagar Sahayak*
GS	*Gram Sabha*
GVA	*Gram Vikas Adhikari*
HSCL	Hindustan Steel Corporation Limited
IARI	Indian Agricultural Research Institute
IAY	*Indira Awas Yojana*
ICRISAT	International Crops Research Institute for the Semi-Arid-Tropics
IEC	Information, Education and Communication
IT	Information Technology
JE	Junior Engineer
JFMC	Joint Forest Management Committee
LWE	Left Wing Extremism
MBC	Most Backward Caste(s)
MGNREGS	Mahatma Gandhi National Rural Employment Guarantee Scheme
MI	Minor Irrigation (works)
MIS	Management Information System
MoEF	Ministry of Environment and Forests
MoRD	Ministry of Rural Development
MoTA	Ministry of Tribal Affairs

MoU	Memorandum of Understanding
MP	Madhya Pradesh
MPDO	Mandal Programme Development Officer
MT	Metric Tonne
NLFT	National Liberation Front of Tripura
NRLM	National Rural Livelihood Mission
NGO	Non-Governmental Organization
NIRD	National Institute of Rural Development (Hyderabad)
NREGA	(Mahatama Gandhi) National Rural Employment Guarantee Act
NREGS	(Mahatama Gandhi) National Rural Employment Guarantee Scheme
OBC	Other Backward Caste
OP	Opening Balance
PD	Project/Programme Director
PMGSY	*Pradhan Mantri Gram Sadak Yojana*
PO	Programme Officer/Project Officer
POS	Point of Sale
POTD	Point of Transaction Device
PRI	Panchayati Raj Institution
PWD	Public Works Department
RES	Rural Engineering Services
RWD	Rural Welfare Department
SC	Scheduled Caste
SDO	Sub-Divisional Officer
SEZ	Special Economic Zone
SGWY	*Swarjayanti Gram Swarozgar Yojana*
SHG	Self-Help Group
SoR	Schedule of Rates
SSS	*Shram Shakthi Sangathan* (in Andhra Pradesh)
ST	Scheduled Tribe
UNDP	United Nations Development Programme
VMC	Village Monitoring Committee

Foreword

Mahatma Gandhi National Rural Employment Guarantee Act (MGNREGA) is a prime flagship programme of the Ministry of Rural Development, Government of India, that directly touches lives of the rural poor and promotes inclusive growth. It has addressed not only the poverty alleviation of the rural households but is also strengthening the livelihood support through enhancing the natural resource base. Though the programme has completed its eight years of implementation, awareness on rights and entitlements among the various stakeholders is still a hurdle. One of the important steps to make MGNREGA a success is the creation of awareness among rural people and other stakeholders. Special emphasis needs to be placed on raising awareness among the MGNREGA workers through several information, education and communication (IEC) methods.

To accomplish the objectives of the MGNREGA, the Government of India has decided to introduce annual awards to be known as Excellence in MGNREGA Administration. The award is envisaged to encourage and acknowledge the outstanding and exemplary contribution made by District MGNREGA Teams in the implementation of NREGA in the country. The State/UT Governments nominate the best-performing districts for the national-level award. The Central Government has been conducting a preliminary verification of the nominations received by it. The eligible nominations are screened by an Expert Committee constituted by the Central Government comprising at least seven eminent persons from the fields of administration, law, management, media, science and technology and academia. The Committee has been chaired by Shri K.B. Saxena, former Secretary, Department of Rural Development, Ministry of Rural Development, and the Joint Secretary of the Department has been acting as the Member-Convenor. The nominees shortlisted by the Central Government were invited to make a presentation before the Expert Committee. Thereafter, the Expert Committee has considered the proposals and also visited the districts for field verification. The Expert Committee has recommended the details of the awardees on the basis of which the Central Government has selected the awardees.

The Expert Committee member has developed district-wise document on their performance based on a few selected indicators. It was felt necessary to circulate these documents of the year 2010–11 among the young district administrators to improve performance of the programme and adapt the suitable best practices for the successful implementation of the wage employment programme.

This volume is a compendium of best cases as well as documentation of the reasons for failure of innovations. This book will be an eye opener for the administrators and provide useful insights into programme implementation for academicians, researchers, scholars, students and policymakers.

Dr M.V. Rao
Director General
National Institute of Rural Development and Panchayati Raj
Ministry of Rural Development
Government of India
Hyderabad

Overview

1.1 PARTICIPATION

Except for Kerala, Panchayati Raj Institutions (PRIs), particularly at the village level, are very weak institutions and their functionality is poor. They suffer from lack of devolution of functions, functionaries and finances. They are unable to resist bureaucratic dictates with regard to the schemes to be taken up, when to start the schemes, the Annual Action Plan (AAP) and labour budget. The decision-making process at the village level was also bureaucracy driven.

Though *panchayat* was a constitutionally empowered body, *sarpanch*s and elected representatives did what the officials desired them to do. Mostly, they were unaware of their autonomy and power. The façade of formalized participation was maintained. *Gram sabha* (GS) meetings were held only when legally required decisions about a programme had to be taken. When held, attendance was very thin and there was hardly an indication of any discussion. The minutes record only one line saying: the following AAP is approved. The AAP was generally prepared by officials.

In some States, choice and prioritization of schemes were determined on the directions of the State Government. In Andhra Pradesh, it was the most centralized of all of them. For example, in 2010–11, it was decided at the State level that only affirmative action programmes of land development should be taken up. The intent was laudable but it compromised the participatory ethos. Elected *panchayat* members, *sarpanch*s, were unable to resist this imposition and internalized this centralization and bureaucratic domination. In fact, they could not resist even directions/suggestions of district officials. Information technology (IT)-enabled interventions also aided this process. Tribal and *dalit sarpanch*s were particularly in fear of officials.

1.2 AWARENESS

The awareness about the programme was limited to two things:

1. an employment opportunity being available under NREGS, and
2. wage rate.

Nowhere did we find the workers being aware about getting employment on demand and being entitled to unemployment allowance. Officials had literally taken away this entitlement simply by not registering work demand. Workers across the States hence only knew that work could be/was taken up under NREGS only when the officials/*panchayat* decided. They did not know they had a right to demand.

Despite six years of implementation of NREGS, still there were pockets where people complained that job cards had not been issued to them. Such persons belonged to the disadvantaged groups (SCs and STs). In many places, there was lack of awareness that a written application had to be filed for demanding work. Usually they made oral request which was not registered.

1.3 PROVISION OF EMPLOYMENT

The greatest weakness/fault line of the MGNREGS implementation across the States was the suppressed demand. There was a huge unmet demand for employment which did not get reflected in official records. The disturbing aspect was that officials everywhere seemed to hold the opposite view that there was no demand for work as people had better employment opportunities elsewhere in private factories/farms, urban areas, etc. It was also claimed that wages were very high in jobs, due to which people were not interested to work in MGNREGS. In all such places, when the team enquired from workers in confidence (not in front of officials), they expressed their desperate need for employment and complained that it was not being provided. Wages on private work/farms were low, they informed. The lower-level bureaucracy was depriving the employment opportunity provided by MGNREGS by not articulating this demand. There was no assertion by the workers due to their powerlessness. Even where they are aware of the provisions, they are scared that officials may deny them employment.

In fact, the AAP and labour budget did not factor in the imperative of providing 100 days of employment to all job card holders. The level of expenditure in the preceding year determined the next year's labour budget.

Workers' demand for employment was nowhere registered genuinely. This was evident from the fact that in none of the places the team visited, when the workers demanded employment was an acknowledgement slip given. What usually happened was that when the officials wanted to start the work they obtained a written request from the workers. This skilfully concealed the time lag between demand for work and its supply and the liability arising therefrom. In this manner, an important feature of demand-based employment that in the event of non-compliance unemployment allowance shall be provided was getting disregarded in most of the States visited.

Overall, the level of employment provided was considerably lower than the entitled 100 days—around 40 days on an average. This level of employment could not ensure livelihood security, particularly for landless agricultural labourers. Even this employment was skewedly distributed among those who participated, further limiting its positive impact.

1.4 WAGE REALIZATION

The workers' entitlement was also affected by low average wage realization against the stipulated MGNREGS wage rate. It was found to be ₹70 to ₹90 as against the minimum wage ranging from ₹120 to ₹150 in different States. Wage calculation was based on the measurement of work performed which was specified in the Schedule of Rates (SoR). Since the SoR was usually applied uniformly, it did not take into account the differing soil/work conditions, especially where the soil was hard, rocky and lacking in moisture. Hence, it turned out to be very adverse to the poor.

There was also a wide gap in the perception of workers about the output of work performed as against the perception of the officials. It became a contentious issue. While the former attributed this discrepancy to measurement which was carried out in their absence and after a lapse of time from the date of its completion, the officials blamed the workers for under-performance.

The SoR had also gone against women workers since work relating to lead and lift usually performed by them was not separately recognized in many places. The result was that even after doing a day's work the average woman worker was hardly able to get the minimum wage stipulated under NREGS.

1.5 PAYMENT OF WAGES

Delay in payment of wages, ranging from a month to several, was observed in each of the States visited because of a variety of reasons. Delay was taking place at each level: at the level of *Rozgar Sahayak*, block office, the engineer, accountant and the bank or post office. Tamil Nadu, where wages were paid in cash, had a better record of payment of wages than the other States visited.

By and large, payment of wages through banks and post offices (rather than cash; except for Tamil Nadu and in Naxalism-affected areas, for instance, Sarguja District, Chhattisgarh) had been universalized. However, workers faced acute problems of delay in payment as bank branches were few (with limited infrastructure capacities) and post offices were helpless because of their guidelines relating to ceiling on handling of cash. Even while they had made payments, many of the banks had not issued passbooks. In the absence of a passbook, it was difficult to verify, as an outsider, whether the wages had been paid or not. It was also difficult for a wage earner to know whether the requisite wage had been credited to his account and when.

1.6 WORKSITE FACILITIES

Worksite facilities such as crèche, shade, drinking water, etc. and provision of work-related equipment were largely missing. In Andhra Pradesh, however, workers were entitled to ₹1 extra wage if they brought their own bottled water. In one State, some cash allowance was also provided for sharpening of tools.

1.7 TIMING OF EMPLOYMENT

The most disturbing aspect observed was that work was not being taken up when it was needed the most. Across the country, the need for work was maximum, immediately after harvest of *rabi* and post-*kharif* sowing of crops. In these months, no on-farm work was available in rural areas. Precisely during these months, we found from job card or work records that no work/programme was taken up. Works under NREGS were not taken up to synchronize with this distress period. The timing of work availability was important. If this was not factored in, the subsequent provisions of work would fail to serve this purpose as the non-availability of work during this lean period forced workers to migrate to distant places.

The most common form of migration was debt-driven employment where a worker received an advance from the contractor and bound himself to work on terms dictated by them. Usually the workers return when rains start. This employment embedded in debt bondage was observed in several places visited (in Maharashtra, Andhra Pradesh, Tamil Nadu, etc.).

NREGS was precisely meant to break this debt-bondage trap which it has not been able to do. If this crucial period of 3–4 weeks was missed, most labourers who had no other source of survival would leave the village. Thus, even if the work was taken up with delay, labourers would not be available. This explains why in the work taken up in this manner, the participation of labourer was low. Officials then interpret this as lack of demand. It required shelf of schemes to be reached well in advance, and other preparatory steps completed to start the work in time. It also required information to be collected from each village about the exploitative networks and the most vulnerable sections of this practice, to target them in the NRGES programme. This was sadly lacking everywhere.

1.8 PLANNING

Planning is a very important aspect of NREGS. In order to provide need-based employment and fulfil programme objectives, a very strong and sound planning was required. It also had to be participatory. This implied that the people in the village had a decisive say in the schemes to be taken up, the timing of taking up the schemes, their prioritization and execution. This participatory planning was nowhere observed.

Panchayat-centric decision making and the provision of a promoter for mobilization of people can be considered to provide input of participation in this exercise. People's participation in implementation was far stronger in Kerala, where before being taken up, schemes were discussed with villagers.

Everywhere else, the entire planning was top down and centralized. GSs hardly had any genuine say.

The schemes taken up were not organically related to the village ecology. For example, isolated land development, water harvesting schemes were planned and implemented without relating them to the watershed. This would impact on their utility, sustainability and cost effectiveness. Even when there was willingness to consider watershed approach, the forest department did not allow ridge areas to be treated as these fell in its domain.

The deficit of planning was also observed in failing to take up certain works (such as land development for Forest Rights Act beneficiaries) in a group so as to realize efficiency of expenditure, effectiveness of area development and optimum utilization of available resources. Planning was reduced to selection of individual beneficiaries rather than area development. Area being conceived here is a tiny cluster which treats all the beneficiaries falling in its unit and covers all aspects of ecological treatment.

Also, where the demand for a scheme was high in a village—as for example, land development of forest *patta* holders—it made no sense to take up one or two *patta* holders in isolation and in different locations. This was exactly what was being done. It would have made sense to take all contiguous *patta* holders together as a compact area.

Financial planning was weak and did not take into account the potential demand with the result that the labour budget itself did not provide for creation of sufficient (100 days) employment. The labour budgets we saw in several places (Pithoragarh, Uttarakhand; Keonjhar, Odisha; Amravati, Maharashtra) would hardly be able to provide 10–15 days of employment per person who had demanded work as against the large number of job card holders requiring work. Hence, at the planning stage itself, the employment entitlement had been severely curtailed.

Low level of labour budget was attributed to low capacity of the *panchayat* to spend. This low capacity was not on account of low demand for work but lack of staff, indifference and insensitivity of officials, lack of sufficient pressure resulting from lower level of awareness (among wage seekers) and lower level of supervision and monitoring. In most places, pockets of tribal habitations suffered from this discrimination.

While all records pointed adherence of 60:40 wage: material ratio guidelines, and the former exceeding the latter, in the field, this proportion appeared fudged. There was a substantive material component entered into the scheme design, and therefore in some places, the information on records and the information on the ground were not in consonance.

Estimates preparation for individual schemes was given a go-by. Standardized estimates were being used rather than keeping local specificities of the area in mind. In some States, there was a standardized estimate (say for land development) which was applicable throughout the district, or even the State. The ceiling was as low as ₹10,000 in some places which led to farcical implementation or what in bureaucratic parlance is called *khanapuri*.

Ecological planning was ignored particularly in relation to dug wells which were taken up in large number quite often within a single village but with no recharge structures constructed (say for instance in Keonjhar District, Odisha). This was evident in not taking into account the level of ground water, not providing for recharge and the sustainability. This would lead to lowering down of water table and drying up of wells.

1.9 QUALITY OF WORKS

The quality of schemes executed in most places was found to be unsatisfactory. The technical input into it was inadequate and suspect in several places. We got the impression that the officials focussed on provision of employment and they tended to overlook qualitative aspects of the schemes.

Quality of works suffered on three counts: (1) design flaws and lack of supervision, (2) incomplete works having been declared completed and closed and (3) standardized estimates of schemes without reference to local site. This led to bad implementation. Programmes approved in a particular year in several places/cases were not started that year. They were taken up later. However, their estimates were not updated creating constraints in their implementation. The earth excavation (*kaccha*) works started late and were not completed before the monsoons leading to silting, water accumulation and even collapse of structures.

Land levelling had been taken up on a large scale in order to fulfil the target of affirmative action programme with little technical input, very low investment and unrelated to the local ecology and watershed approach. It lacked both conceptual and engineering aspects besides being poorly executed. There was widespread absence of compacting the loose earth piled on the embankment, provision of side slope, cross drainage in water storage or harvesting schemes. In land development schemes in several places, the schemes were reduced to top soil removal, *medh* (bund) formation and some slope ceiling. The schemes failed to take up cases in a cluster to integrate the area appropriately in the watershed, both for cost efficiency, use effectiveness and optimum benefits. Equity issues were also ignored in selection of beneficiaries. The assets being created on account of poor quality of works left much to be desired in terms of utility, durability, cost effectiveness and productivity.

1.10 GOVERNANCE

Governance problems were encountered in all States which constrained the implementation of the programme and adversely affected the wage seekers. Governance is the most crucial factor in implementation of NREGS. Dedicated structures of implementation have been provided in the programme guidelines such as a full-fledged *Rojgar Sahayak* at the *panchayat* level and a project officer at the block level. Engineering staff has also been provided to assist them. There is a team of officials at the district level and Technical Resource Support group at the State level. The time-bound processes of scheme approval and measurement have been provided.

In none of the States visited, except Kerala where the *panchayat*s are very well-equipped in terms of staff, was the full range of this dedicated staff available. As a result, each functionary at the *panchayat* had to handle a large jurisdiction. There was huge shortage of staff at all levels. There were vacancies which had not been filled for months. Tribal blocks and *panchayat*s suffered the most from paucity of staff. These areas also faced unwillingness of officials posted there to work and stay in the area. These areas also suffered from lack of adequate roads, phone connectivity and public transport; neither was a transport allowance given to staff posted there. The contractual nature of appointments of most staff at lower levels created insecurity and lack of motivation. Newly appointed staff members were sent to the area without prior training or exposure to NREGS. Many of them had no idea how to maintain records and what to inspect.

Technical support to the NREGS programme in several places visited was inadequate which impacted the quality of schemes. Even though administrative cost is well provided for under the 6% administrative expenditure, provision of adequate staff has suffered due to a number of factors including delay in recruitment and reluctance of those recruited to join. The tribal areas are the worst affected in this regard.

A substantial portion of the NREGS funds has been directly assigned to line departments such as Irrigation, Forest, Agriculture and PWD. It was observed that line departments did not accept the discipline of NREGS and the District Programme Officer (DPO) was unable to bring them in line. The line departments function independent of the GP and refuse to follow NREGS guidelines regarding linkage with *panchayats*. Nowhere did we find line department taking GS approval for schemes, submitting their estimates or information to the *panchayat*, or even furnishing muster rolls to them. They dealt with the District Programme Office directly and funds too were transferred to them at this level. Therefore, the process of implementation laid down, participation of wage seekers and accountability to the *panchayat* had been undermined.

PRIs have been undermined in other ways too. While the GP is the most effective decision-making structure in the NREG Act, all the records were kept at the block level. In many places, even the Management Information System (MIS) of *panchayat* was not available at the *panchayat* level. In such a situation, what kind of control it could exercise is easy to understand.

The extensive data generated by the MIS provides a useful evidence to identify fault-lines in the NREGS implementation. However, little use was made of this information at the block level or below, to make corrective interventions. This underlined the need for imparting training on how to make use of/interpret data of the MIS to improve the performance and address inequities.

1.11 ACCOUNTABILITY

Vigilance committees have been formed but nowhere functional. Similarly, grievance redressal mechanism in most of the States visited do not exist at all. However, in some States where it is there, it exists at the district level (rather than at the village level).

There were blank registers in village *panchayats* wherever we visited. It was evident that complaints were not formally registered. This is important because people usually make oral complaints. At the district level too, complaints received were very few if at all, and no credible effort was made to pursue/cross-check compliance.

Andhra Pradesh was the sole exception where social audits were regularly carried out twice a year, though the entire process is bureaucracy driven. Action was taken against erring officials where financial irregularities were detected and money misappropriated realized. While action is also taken by State Governments against erring officials in case of such complaints, this was not with reference to social audit findings.

In other States where a half-hearted beginning was made to have social audits carried out, it was a one-off affair in some places or once a year and that too entrusted to a non-governmental organization (NGO). It did not come up with any disfunctionality. The routinized reports of such social audits with no shortcomings observed made them farcical. There was no regularity either. It did not show any participation. The ambit of social audit even in Andhra Pradesh did not cover the phenomenon of unmet demand.

On the whole, the implementation of social audit has not really taken off.

1.12 EQUITY

Huge inequities were observed in the implementation of the programme. These operated between blocks, between *panchayats* and between villages. These inequities were reflected in distribution of works, allocation of resources, generation of employment, number of persons with 100 days of work, level of expenditure, completion and execution of schemes and affirmative action programmes.

This disparity is most marked in respect of GPs and blocks with tribal concentration which are also constrained by lack of adequate staff and other infrastructure (banks, post offices, road connectivity and transport facilities). Additionally, there is also reluctance of staff to work in these areas. These factors, in turn, affect implementation of NREGS and cause/perpetuate inequities. The programme, far from bridging gaps in reaching of development benefits, has rather reinforced them.

There were intra-group inequities as well in the selection of beneficiaries for affirmative action programmes and for convergence of subsidy-oriented programmes of other line departments (Forest, Fisheries, etc.). In the selection of beneficiaries, no objective and transparent mode was in place. Elites in the community managed to corner benefits of subsidized schemes while a large number of others and more deserving ones failed to attract notice. The selection of beneficiary was usually influenced by local officials' preferences.

Cancellation of job cards (non-renewal) emerged as a new weapon of exclusion and inequity. The large-scale exclusion of those who had failed to report for work in the past was the most glaring form of inequity where SCs/STs were involved and their number in this list was substantial. The officials failed to go into reasons for their absence and appreciate the gravity of damage it caused them. The isolate cases of non-issue of job cards largely belonged to the marginalized sections. Inequities in availing of the work opportunity under NREGS, realizing optimum wage admissible, completing 100 days of work, observed across the country, are an offshoot of factors over which workers have no control and which they are unable to bridge. *The important point is that these inequities are not even noticed and far less addressed.*

1.13 GOOD PRACTICES

In Alappuzha District (Kerala), advance payment after closure of the muster roll (without measurement) helped in reducing delay in payments. Also, a project diary containing details of the project sanctioned, implementation milestones, list of equipment to be used by labourer and rental charges receivable on equipment by wage seekers was used by mates. The diary also provides for workers' comments and observations by visiting/inspecting officers. In Thrissur District (Kerala), a pre-execution project meeting with households demanding work—to generate awareness among villagers about NREGS, and work to be executed— was observed.

In Andhra Pradesh, as informed by officials, SC and ST job card holders could avail more than 100 days of work in times and areas of drought. The additional funds came from the State exchequer. Also, in the closing two months of 2011–12 financial year, the State was concentrating on providing wage labour to SCs and STs. It was also informed that preference was given to SC, ST and landless in opening of all NREGS works in the State. Besides, a *Shram Shakthi Sangathan* (SSS) group had complete freedom to organize employment for 100 days for members of its group, implying availability of work on demand. In some GPs visited in Andhra Pradesh, there were separate SSSs for disabled workers. Such people were not only involved in NREGS work with other groups but also given 30% extra allowance in their wages. During peak summers, an extra allowance and in drought-prone areas higher wages for NREGS work had been permitted. In Vizianagaram District, the field assistant, *panchayat* secretary and *sarpanch* jointly identified and approved NREGS works in their GP.

The SSS system in Andhra Pradesh and SC/ST promoter in Kerala had helped in mobilizing labourers and people from disadvantaged communities for NREGS work. The SSS system had broken the stranglehold of FAs by neutralizing their power and effectively arrested bogus mustering. However, it was not uniformly successful. For instance, while in Vizianagaram District it had achieved good results, it had made no dent in Nizamabad District where NREGS work was abysmally low and exclusion of marginalized was glaring.

In one district, a fixed amount per day was paid for workers for bringing their own basket and for drinking water.

In Dhar District, change in cropping pattern by taking up commercial crops without entirely giving up traditional crops was in evidence.

In Thrissur, measurement sticks are given to wage groups to know the quantum of work generated by them.

Salem District (Tamil Nadu) had generated unique MIS data, whereby a break-up of man-days worked by each social category households (i.e. caste-wise for SC/ST/OBC/General) registered under NREGS, against the number of total households in that village, was available to officials. However, the data which pointed to large-scale exclusion of SCs/STs in issue of job cards and they are getting much less employment than OBC and General category groups were not noticed by them for making corrective interventions.

1.14 WOMEN EMPOWERMENT

Work rate participation of women was impressive in southern and hilly States. In Tamil Nadu and Kerala, most of the NREGS workers were women. There was a high demand for NREGS work from them. Tamil Nadu also showed a high degree of participation of older people. It was observed that women workers were more considerate towards older persons among them in shouldering additional work where their output was lagging.

Despite high degree of women participation, it was not reflected in the nature of schemes taken up. There is neither greater nor assertive participation of women in the GS nor projection of specific schemes that would benefit them. The participating women have perceived NREGS as an employment- and income-generating opportunity and not as an instrument of empowerment and improving the quality of their lives.

Surprisingly, the only observed women-friendly initiative came from the Collector, Pithoragarh

District (Uttarakhand), who started the production of green fodder for free distribution to reduce the drudgery and risk of collecting it as it was largely done by women. Regrettably, the scheme suffered from other inequities. Had it been encouraged on *panchayat* land with women participation and equitable benefit sharing, it would have huge potential to empower women.

However, in terms of nature of schemes taken up, no gender sensitivity was observed anywhere. Even where *sarpanch*s were women, there was no thrust on schemes which reduced their drudgery or empowered them in other ways.

Absence of women mates on the worksite was a glaring omission in this respect. Also, we did not come across instances where women actively participated in GS meetings or took initiative to suggest schemes.

1.15 IMPACT OF THE PROGRAMME

It is usually believed (and as many DPOs claimed) that MGNREGS has reduced migration within area. In the places visited, we did not find this claim to be true. Migration was still taking place, and on a large scale. This is because when labourers/the poor need work desperately and it is not available under NREGS, they have no option but migrate (to find livelihood elsewhere).

The overall impression we have gathered is that work is not available on demand and in particular, during the lean season. In many places, payment is not made on time. The poor have little staying capacity and move whenever work is available. Usually, the contractors take them away precisely at such a time by paying them an advance.

The number of person-days of work generated under NREGS is far below even the entitled 100 days and is not sequenced to cover major part of the worst period when there is no farm work in the village. It is not equitably distributed among the jobseekers to ensure sustainability. Work provision is not made across the year by consciously blanking out nearly six months from NREGS operation so as to facilitate diversion of labour to private farmers.

The objective of the programme that at all times, option of NREGS work should be available to a worker to choose between NREGS and other work opportunities was not served as such an opportunity was not being provided. While this broadly sums up the overall picture, some team members found two to three instances where some households were able to avert migration due to work

availed or facilities provided by NREGS, unlike in the preceding year. For instance, in Panvi Madai GP of Periyanaichanpalayam Block and Mathanpatty GP of Thunna Munthur Block in Coimbatore District, some workers who used to migrate earlier were staying back now on account of work being available under NREGS. Decline in migration was also observed in Dhar District and reduction (in migration) in Nalanda District on account of availability of irrigation facilities.

The team did not find any evidence of non-availability of labourers to private farmers as a result of operation of NREGS. This is because during the agricultural season, usually no NREGS works are taken up. Our enquiry from the agricultural labourer also did not suggest that their wage level on private farmers' land had increased. Rather, the level of wages received continued to be lower than NREGS in the absence of better options and weak bargaining capacity due to their vulnerable position.

NREGS work has had a positive impact in terms of dignity it has given them and a little assertion at times in a given situation. The positive impact on women and elderly workers is more marked. Without exception they preferred NREGS work to engagement on private farms.

In terms of environmental impact, implementing officials claimed larger capacity to conserve water wherever schemes relating to construction and deepening of water bodies had been completed before monsoon. Nanded District (Maharashtra), faced with acute scarcity of drinking water, had a major focus on water resource planning. NREGS works had reduced the demand for water tankers, as claimed. In Nalanda District (Bihar), the revival of traditional water harvesting structures had provided surface water for irrigation and reduced reliance on ground water which had helped officials to reduce diesel subsidy for operation of pump sets provided to farmers, as informed. *Both the above evidences were, however, anecdotal.*

1.16 SUGGESTIONS

The following suggestions are recommended:

i. A massive effort is required to bring centre-stage primacy of *panchayats*/GSs in decision making and participation of MGNREGS workers, particularly the SCs/STs/women therein. This should receive priority attention.

ii. Strong directives should be sent to States against non-renewal of job cards on grounds of job card holder not reporting for work in the previous years. The most vulnerable of the rural poor are the greatest victims of this zeal for exclusion.

iii. Timing, sufficiency and sequencing of provision of work and availability of work throughout the year are necessary to prevent distress migration. These parameters of employment should be settled through focussed and sustained discussion in the GS.

iv. Awareness creation and mobilization of workers, particularly of *dalits/adivasi*s, should be a continuing process and pursued through multiple approaches. The SSS innovation in Andhra Pradesh and mobilizer of workers institutionalized in Kerala are mechanisms worth pursuing in other States.

v. The procedure for registering demand for work and getting acknowledgement for it should be made worker- and situation-friendly and empowering. Mechanisms for registering demand (made orally) should also be provided.

vi. Priority to and capacity building for planning of MGNREGS need to be pursued aggressively. The dimensions of planning should include, among others, financial, ecological, productive asset building, timely provision of employment, starting and completion of schemes, local resources utilization, timely procurement of material, etc.

vii. Work norms for payment of wages should be insisted upon. Payment without reasonable output of work should be strongly discouraged or curbed.

viii. A major effort needs to be made to improve technical supervision in designing, estimate preparation and implementation of schemes. This should be pursued through training, preparation of manual of schemes and its circulation, dissemination of case studies of flawed schemes, etc.

ix. Timely payment of wages through banks and post offices continues to be a formidable problem. This should be addressed over a long run by opening of branches/sub-branches/ Regional Rural Banks and post office units.

   a. In the short run, banks should be persuaded to disburse wages on a fixed day at *panchayat* head quarters with security and vehicle provided by the district administration.

   b. Capacity of post offices to handle cash should be augmented.

x. Social audit should be institutionalized, to start with, on the pattern of Andhra Pradesh with greater capacity building of non-official team members and ambit of audit extending to all areas of concerns to the MGNREGS and not confined to financial irregularities and omissions and commissions of staff.

xi. Geographical isolation of tribal blocks/ *panchayat*s, leading to social exclusion as reflected in the poor implementation of MGNREGS, should be neutralized by issuing a set of directions which ensure availability of sufficient staff, their mandatory stay in rural areas, mobility, training, adequate financial allocation, ensuring participation of beneficiaries, and especially capacity building of tribal *sarpanch*s and ward members who require substantial training particularly to develop confidence and assertion so as to remove their sense of fear of officials.

xii. Centralization in decision making on scheme selection, even if it is for public good and social justice, should be strongly discouraged as it completely erodes local participation and primacy of *panchayat*s and GSs.

xiii. MIS should also be developed on performance in respect of institutional measures for enforcing accountability—vigilance committees, ombudsman and supervision of schemes. Use of IT for monitoring of implementation and tracking down bottlenecks for timely intervention is also reinforcing centralization and weakening the capacity of local officials and structures to intervene quickly to address problems. Its use needs to be recalibrated to strengthen decentralization.

xiv. Innovative ways should be thought of for ensuring effective participation of women in GS meetings and discussion on selection of schemes in order that schemes of particular interest to them are prioritized. A tentative list of such schemes could also be prepared and circulated. A sizable number of women workers should be selected as mates.

xv. Widespread inequities—inter-block, inter-*panchayat*, intra-*panchayat* and between social groups in performance of MGNREGS, such as provision of employment, allocation of funds and their utilization, availability of staff, number of schemes started and completed, etc.—need to be bridged through monitoring focussed specifically on this dimension and timely intervention. MIS should be effectively used to identify such inequities. Officials need to be sensitized on this issue.

xvi. Autonomy of line departments from accountability to *panchayat*s should be strongly discouraged. They should get schemes approved by GS, seek its view on schemes to be taken up, announce the time and venue of starting work in advance and submit muster rolls and scheme records to the *panchayat*s.

xvii. The incidence of low wage realization despite a day's hard work needs to be addressed by:

a. Group measurement of schemes immediately after completion to remove suspicion of under-measurement and incidence of delayed measurement.

b. Appropriate revision of SoR taking into account nature and texture of soil and making provision of lead and lift, where not included.

xviii. The Ministry of Rural Development (MoRD) should address difficulties faced by local officials in taking up works in forest areas and persuade the Ministry of Environment and Forests (MoEF) to issue necessary directions in this regard. The MoRD and the Ministry of Tribal Affairs (MoTA) should vigorously pursue implementation of the Forest Rights Act to address the indifference of district officials and utilization of MGNREGS for productive utilization of land that STs occupy.

xix. Convergence of MGNREGS with other development programmes, wherever effected, has been confined to provision of irrigation, inputs for horticulture and fisheries, and is therefore limited to households having land holdings. Its wider potential for benefitting landless persons and forging lateral linkage with other programmes needs to be stressed with examples of how it can be done.

xx. Maintenance of records is getting increasingly de-prioritized by the concerned officials. This includes making entries in job cards and bank pass books, besides various registers. Also, job cards are taken away by officials on various pretexts and kept with them for months. Higher officials also do not monitor this aspect and do not inspect records during their visit. Regular monitoring of the state of record maintenance needs to be insisted upon.

The MGNREGS: a theme-wise report

2.1 PROCESSES OF IMPLEMENTATION

The *panchayat*, the lowest of the three-tiered decentralized governance structure, is a constitutionally empowered body of elected representatives which has been assigned the most crucial function of planning and implementation of MGNREGS under the Act. This empowerment has been purposely done so as to ensure that people's needs are adequately addressed. However, this objective remains unrealized because nowhere did we feel that the *sarpanch* was carrying out his/her duties as per the wishes of the people. He/she and other elected representatives more or less seemed to function as per the dictates of the officials. Tribal and *dalit sarpanch*s were particularly in fear of them.

Selection of schemes appeared to be completely determined by the officials, than elected representatives suggesting them. In fact, *panchayat* functionaries seemed to have internalized what officials told them. It did not seem that they knew that they had the power to initiate proposals and even to overrule official advice if informally given. As it was found across districts, attendance in *gram sabha* (GS) as per qorums was there but there were no instances of genuine discussions. The decisions in the meetings were more like announcement of proposals initiated and desired by officials. They seemed to sponsor schemes to which *panchayat* members/villagers simply agreed. While formalized participation was shown through minutes of meeting in the GS register, as conversations with them indicated, there was no discussion or contestation by people. There were no disagreements, alternative suggestions or qualitative comments. The final minutes on record which blandly indicated approval of schemes could have only come from officials.

At several places, there was immense possibility of taking up schemes on land development and water bodies, which collectively benefit the village community. Sadly, discussions on these kinds of alternative proposals were lacking.

In Kakna GP (Surguja District, Chhattisgarh), in a meeting with villagers, *panchayat* functionaries and officials, the investigation officers were told how the *sarpanch* (a tribal) was so scared of officials that he refused to pay any heed to the views of the people and victimized them if they complained. Villagers also seemed to have given up. As one of them said: 'Inse ladenge to humein kuch denge hi nahin. Jo ooncha bolega usey kuch nahin milega'. (If we fight with the officials or raise our voices against them, they will not give us the benefit of government schemes/programmes.) They told the officers how the names of some people (who had complained against officials) were struck off from the list of housing [perhaps *Indira Awas Yojana* (IAY)] beneficiaries. Another of them said: *Main dar ke maare isliye nahin boltaa hoon ki meraa naam cut jayegaa, mujhe kuch nahin milega*. [I do not speak out of fear because my name would be struck off (from the list of beneficiaries) and I would get nothing.] In this village, around 50–60 people regularly migrated to Ambikapur in search of work as no work was available in the village.

In Andhra Pradesh, centralized and computerized system of NREGS implementation, apparently initiated to monitor programme performance, had in effect eroded space for participation of the district machinery and the *panchayat*s. The choice of schemes, release of funds, submission of musters, verification, payment, etc. were all online, State-led and based in Hyderabad, leaving no scope for any initiative or questioning by the *panchayat*. In fact, there was lack of diversity in schemes and shelf of works was restricted to few. Works of priority for a particular year were decided at State level and applied across the State through a centralized direction. For example, the single focus during last two years was schemes relating to water bodies [minor irrigation (MI) tank, etc.]. The next priority was land development and accordingly such schemes were identified in every village. Also, transfer of funds was online from State to district level. From the district, wage transfer was made to the *mandal*, and then subsequently to the post office. In fact, it was only the uploading of information which was decentralized.

In Dhalai District (Bagmara *panchayat*, Tripura), a telling evidence pointing to clear lack of people's participation in GS meetings was that GS proceedings were recorded in English. Obviously, the *panchayat* secretary, a government official, wrote it. Officials defended it as they said it was the official language of the State. Also, the attendance of each GS meeting was not recorded below the proceedings but in a separate register. Even the muster rolls, which every labourer has a right to see, were recorded in English in the district.

In Talegaaon GP of Amravati District (Maharashtra), it was informed that the GS does not pass labour budget. It is proposed and communicated by officials. A telling evidence of official insensitivity towards MGNREGS was that while there were 1,379 job card holders, 900 of them being SCs and mostly landless, only two days of employment had been provided during 2010–11 and the labour budget was only 9 lakh. Officials routinely defended this low provision of work on grounds of lack of demand, which everywhere turned out to be false as there was huge unmet need for work.

Then there was an instance in one GP of Salem District where the *panchayat* had passed a resolution on taking up desilting work of a village pond. This had been encroached upon by a powerful person from the community and the *panchayat* had passed a resolution for evicting him. However, despite representations at the block level, their resolution was not acted upon and consequently work had not begun. This kind of inaction disempowers *panchayat*s. Since there was a dispute, it would have required coordination with other departments at the block or district level, say the *Tehsildar*, who would have to take out the survey number and inspect the area to settle the dispute. At the district level, there is a need to collect information on those resolutions passed by the *panchayat*s which require action at the district administration level on priority basis, especially the ones which require coordinated effort of different departments, say water supply, irrigation, revenue, highways, agriculture, etc.

In Jhilpi, a single village GP of Maleghat region (Amravati District, Maharashtra), the inspecting officers came across an unusual case of a newly elected *sarpanch* continuing to hold his previous post of *Gram Rogzar Sahayak* (GRS)! He was still having job cards of villagers and had not handed over charge to another person ever since his election to the GP. Because of this reason, no work had been initiated in this village for the last four months. In Nizamabad District, the *panchayat* bodies had been dissolved, so there was no work for the last two months.

In Vizianagaram District, where emphasis was on providing 100 days of assured wage employment, a good practice was that the field assistant, *panchayat* secretary and *sarpanch* jointly identified and approved NREGS works in their GP.

Across States, *panchayat*s were totally marginalized when it came to schemes being implemented by line departments. They had no information on their schemes sanctioned, or being taken up for execution. In fact, NREGS money was being directly transferred to line departments and their total budget possibly had a substantial share of NREGS funds. They did not report to the *panchayat* but directly to the District Programme Coordinator (DPC). And since the district did not inform the *panchayat*s, they were clueless about what was happening in the works taken up under NREGS by them. No muster rolls or fund utilization details were shared with the *panchayat*s. An anguished official in Sarguja told the visiting team how despite repeated requests/intimations, forest department officials never attended a GS meeting. '*Bulaane par peon bhej dete hain. Na koi soochnaa dete hain, na koi report dete hain*' (On being invited, they send their department's peon to the meeting. Neither do they provide any information or send us any report), the visiting team was told. Agency or line departments were also not following NREGS norms in filling up of job cards. It is important that not only the line department inform the *panchayat* in advance about the work being started, but also take their approval. Sarguja District, however, empowered *panchayat*s by assigning a larger share of funds.

There was a need for training and capacity building of elected *panchayat* officials with respect to budget preparation, provisioning of 100 days of work and its timely sequencing to prevent migration, planning of land development and water management schemes and maintenance of records, participation of members, monitoring of implementation of schemes and timely payment, etc. Because of low awareness levels and execution capacity, they were easily taken in by officials' arguments and did not assert their views. This was weakening the entire PRI system.

2.2 PROVISION OF EMPLOYMENT

Across the districts, there was an immense demand and urgent need of work. However, the number of days work provided was not only very small but there was no continuity in provisioning of work.

In Nalanda District (Bihar), though the employment provided in the district increased from 38.80 lakh person-days during 2009–10 to 45.66 lakh person-days in 2010–11 (18% increase), it was too inadequate as during the lean employment season, landless agricultural labourers migrate to Patna and various destinations outside the State for livelihood in the absence of work in the village. The issue apparently has never been discussed in the GS. In Madhavpura Bazar GP of Chandi Block, wage seekers opt to work in brick kilns, where the family works for a piece-rated wage of ₹200–250 per day than for a minimum wage in NREGS. This is not on account of preference for brick kiln work but due to lack of adequate and timely employment. On an average, only 10–12 days of employment is provided per household in the district despite a sizeable population of SCs and agriculture labourers belonging to other communities.

In Nanded District (Maharashtra), the share of SCs in total person-days generated was 16%, STs' share was 9% and women's share was 47%. Based on the job cards issued, the person-days generated per household among SCs was eight days and STs nine days. In total, it was only nine days. This indicates that there is a huge unmet demand among the households who have received the job cards. It was also found in few GPs that the job cards were not issued in continuous serial numbers. In the website, the last job card number is considered to count the number of job cards issued. In Pasaad *gram* of Nanded Block, the women group informed that most of them did not have job cards and they were desperate to get employment during the lean season.

In Salem District, job cards were assigned to each individual member of a family and while the numbering enabled to identify members of one family (same number with A, B, C extension), it seemed difficult to monitor a household completing 100 days of work. However, officials did mention of a separate register being maintained at the *panchayat* level to keep track of the number of days worked by an individual household.

A stock explanation offered by NREGS officials across states was that there was no demand for work as private work (in agricultural fields, mills, factories, etc.) was not only readily available but also the wages were much higher (almost double of NREGS rates, going by the figures officials quoted). This was certainly a lie, told with impunity, by officials in each of the States visited. Conversations with labourers clearly indicated that this was not true. The only instance of market wages getting increased was reported in Dhamoli village in Nalanda District.

Not only was outside labour work scarce, wages on private agricultural fields, especially on lands of big landed farmers, were exploitatively low. They were unfailingly much lesser than NREGS wage rate in all the places we visited except in Thrissur, Kerala, where it was reported to be higher. In fact, in Keonjhar District (Odisha) and Telengana region of Nizamabad (Andhra Pradesh), it was as low as ₹60 per day compared to NREGS rate of ₹129 per day. In Harshal GP (Dharni Block) of Amravati, agriculture wages were ₹60 per day. Work availability was a problem, and everywhere workers conveyed that they would prefer NREGS work to a work on private farm or as a migrant worker, even if the wage was higher. The reason for non-availability of NREGS work during agricultural season (June–November) was due to the pressure exerted by big farmers—more or less across States—on implementing officials for not opening NREGS work in order that cheap labour was available to them. There were other reasons too, as stated elsewhere in this report. The end result was that the government machinery in States had failed in providing wage employment even for half of the number of 100 days.

In places where work was provided, it was not spread over the year, and there were lean seasons, say post-harvest, when no farm work was available which forced labourers to either migrate to cities in search of work or enter in debt-linked employment (which also meant going for work in other States for long periods of time). To benefit large and medium land owners, work was altogether stopped for several months (June to October). In Chhattisgarh, a government circular clearly instructed not to initiate earth work under NREGS during June to September/October. On the ground, this had been enforced by not taking up any work under MGNREGS at all for several months.

Even in the months when work was provided, there was uneven distribution among the job card holders. In Vellukara village (Thrissur), women workers working on a drain (leading to an irrigation channel) cleaning work, told the visiting team that on an average 15–20 days in a month, both men and women were without work and income.

In Kaapadkheda village (Amravati District), where there were 244 job card holders, and 20% of the people landless, only four days of work, which began some days ago, had been provided in the current year. Last year, work on a field road had begun, which lay unfinished (*adhooraa*) now. 'We took up four to five works. No one comes for work', officials told the visiting team. 'We even did a *munaadi* (drum beating)'. Villagers had something else to say though. They informed that the work was not started when they needed it most. As a result, they had to migrate. The contractor paid them an advance and took them away for a specified period. They had no option but to accept this debt bondage.

It was observed that landless people made both ends meet by doing labour work outside the village or by working in other people's homes in the village. All they could manage was just 15 days of work in a month. After Holi, there was even less work. Champubala Nareskar, a farm labourer, told the visiting team that ₹60 was agricultural wage on farmer's fields (in comparison to ₹127, the wage rate for NREGS work) and officials were bold enough to say that no one came for work here. In nearby Davida village, '*Padey rehtey hain. Kaam to mila nahin, varshon se nahin. Nahin to hum kyon nahin karte?*' a villager said on being asked about employment under NREGS (We sit idle. Since years, we have not got work. Or else why would not we do it?). People earned ₹50 by working on other people's agricultural fields. In fact, this was the prevalent rate in entire Maleghat, one of the poorest regions of India in Amravati District of Maharashtra.

In Paatna village (Narmada District, Gujarat), no work was undertaken last year. 'Agricultural work in fields is easily available here, so people don't come for NREGS', officials told the visiting team, adding: '*Patelon kaa khet hai, kaam miltaa hai*' (People get work on the fields of Patels). As stated elsewhere, the wage rate in such work (in cotton/*kapaa* fields) ranged around ₹60 (whereas NREGS offered ₹110). In tribal areas of Keonjhar District (Odisha), villagers spent a day in collecting firewood, and then walking eight hours the other day to sell it in the nearest *haat* (village weekly/monthly market). Their earnings after spending two days and walking around 20 km were a princely sum of ₹100. Here too, during village visit, officials said there was no demand for work, until the visitors got to know of the truth on interacting with the villagers. In fact, in Keonjhar, a district known for hunger deaths, three days' average work in a year was generated.

In Dokaseela village of Parvathipuram GP (Vizianagaram District), which had 336 SCs and 693 STs, payment of six weeks' work had been pending for over 21 days. NREGS or forest department work was not available for almost 10–20 days in a month. At this stressful time, they went to the forest to pick leaves and sell firewood. Their earnings were ₹30 per day.

In several of the districts visited, the visiting team came across instances of passbook being kept in custody of officials (*sarpanch, Rozgar Sahayak*, etc.) or post office for some vague reason or the other. In Paatna village (Narmada District), when the visiting team visited the *basti* of (perhaps SCs) which had houses constructed under the IAY, the officers were informed that their job cards were in the *panchayat* as these had been taken by the *Talhati*. When the officers asked the *sarpanch* about the job cards, he said that the Branch Post Master of the post office had taken these for the last three months, without giving a reason for it. In Pithoragarh, instance of job cards being with the *Pradhan* was observed.

In Naagudhana village (Daavida GP, Narmada District), a villager told us: '*Job card milaa, sahib logon ne jabt kar liya*'. (We got our job cards, but these were confiscated by government officials.) In Keonjhar, a tribal district, the visiting team was told about the *sarpanch* keeping all the job cards of poor Juaang tribals. In Mahulpara here, where literally no work was taken up during 2010–11, the job cards of several persons had been lying with the *Gram Sanyojak* for the past six months. In other places too, job cards seemed to have been taken away from them by the *Gram Sanyojak* (who had a tight control on the programme) as people in several blocks told the visiting team about it. Nowhere did higher officials try to investigate reasons or understand the dynamics of exploitation to which lower government officials seemed party to. In the forest village (sanctuary areas) of Narmada, people openly complained that their job cards had been taken away by the forest department officials (Kokti, Sissa, Geechad villages). In Pithoragarh District of Uttarakhand too, job cards were by and large with the *Pradhan* and the workers were largely clueless about the number of days they had worked and amount they had earned.

In Thrissur District of Kerala, overall mandays generated were low, as also the fact that most NREGS works undertaken were largely of short durations, say of around two weeks. In Thamarachaal, a tribal village with a single crop area, a total of only 19 days of work had been provided during 2011–12. Also, *as against work demanded, work provision was very low*. For instance, one woman had demanded 14 days of work during June–July against which only three days had been provided. Payments in passbooks reflected work for two weeks in one go indicating the mismatch in oral statement of labourer and the passbook details. People here were in urgent need of work, which was yet to begin. In Taamravaylachaar village of Panacherry GP, where people were agitating for work, job cards showed three to four days of work for the entire year. For this village, which had 209 job cards, the average days of work provided per person during 2010–11 was six days. In the same year, while it had a budget of ₹88 lakh, only ₹58 lakh was spent, implying 40% unspent funds. In one of the villages (perhaps Anjansingi) in Dhamangaon Block (Amravati District), an average of eight days of work was generated and the money spent was ₹10.44 lakh. Out of 1,379 labourers, only 45 got employment.

Across the States, one could sense that genuine demand for work was getting suppressed. In Thrissur District, the visitor officers were told, nearly 60% job cards including those of SCs had been slashed in 2011–12—either cancelled or not renewed, on the ground that wage seekers had not participated in work in the last three years. In Vellangalur Block (which had four villages including Vellukura which had higher share of SCs and STs), nearly 75% job cards had been cancelled. While the number of job cards was 2,848 in 2010–11, it was 799 in 2011–12. The reasons for not attending the work may be non-availability of work, timing of opening work after labour had migrated and delay in payment of wages. The reality from field visit interaction with villagers was contrary to records which indicated that the number of persons employed was very low and that only 25% of job card holders were demanding work. This requires further investigation. In fact, in Vellukura, the number of job card holders (799) almost matched with the number of persons who demanded work (743).

In Alappuzha District, participation of men is low primarily because they prefer to/engage in other types of work while women come up for NREGS work. The labour market seems to be segregated along gender lines.

In Tadkole village of Banswada *mandal* (Nizamabadad District), people with passbooks in their hands mobbed the team, demanding work. 'There are a large number of labourers here, that is why they are not providing us work', wage seekers told the visiting team. 'People are not coming for work,' the field assistant had told the visiting team just earlier. The distress in the eyes of the people was disturbing. In fact, in this district, nearly 200 persons' wages had been pending since two to four years

on account of double count (job card). While the government knew it and the problem was being attended to, it had created a groundswell of anger and frustration among people. Because of this reason, people were not reporting for work and work was not being taken up. In this region, April–May (after the crop is harvested) was the worst period in terms of work availability. '*Bekaari mein rehte hain*, city (Hyderabad) *mein jaate hain*' (They stay unemployed, go to the city), people told the visiting team in one of the *mandals*.

In Amravati District, in certain GPs, officials at the *panchayat* level were putting a precondition that labourers should come as a group to demand work (*Aap pehle group banaiye, phir kaam denge*) and individuals would not be included in NREGS works being undertaken or sanctioned by them. Under the Act, there is no such condition for providing work.

In Nizamabad District, in several GPs, the new rule allowing a *Shram Shakti Sangthan* (SSS) group worker to participate in more than one NREGS work was still not widely known. The old rule of one work per group was being followed as a result of which mates were not demanding work and workers were not getting wage work. There was a huge communication gap. Demand for work was there, people were willing to work, yet no work was being taken up. As workers told the visiting team in Chinna Rampur *tanda* of STs: '*Ye impression thaa ki kaam nahin le sakte hain, isliye kaam nahin huaa*' [The impression was that work (more than one per group) could not be taken up, that is why no work was started]. Officials and FAs also kept them in the dark when they went to ask for NREGS work. '*Aaegaa to bataaenge*' (When work is allowed, we'll inform you), they said.

In Khaarigaaon, a tribal village (Saalai GP) in Maleghat region of Amravati District, work had not been taken up (except one which got opened recently) and workers were sitting idle, though desperately in need of work. Here 50% people went out in search of work. A woman doing quilt work told that it fetched her ₹20 per day. Here, nearly 50 persons did not have job cards, and payment of 65–70 persons was pending since one year. Across villages, it was told that no work was being taken up. '*Karmachari nahin chaahte ki vikaas ho*', they said (Government officials do not want that development happens in our villages). In Pedagulla GP (Nizamabad District), workers told that sufficient work was not taken up last year as a result of which several of them had to go to Hyderabad for three months in summer for getting wage work. In another GP (Khandaballur), it was observed that while job cards showed work entry (which appeared to be recently entered) for the month of July 2011, the cumulative number of days worked in the previous years were incorrect. Probably wrong data was being entered. This needed to be looked into.

In Khoda Amba, a forest village (Ambavadi GP) in Narmada District (a Phase I district), while no work was undertaken last year, in the current financial year (2011–12) work was undertaken for the first time in December. '*Pehli baar kaam niklaa hai*' (For the first time work has been taken up), villagers informed the visiting team. While some said road work from the village to the cremation ground took place in May–June (of which no entry was made in the job card), the fact of the matter was also that 110 of the 120 households in the village were landless and most of them went to Ankaleshwar and Surat in search of work.

In Daavida village of Maleghat region of Amravati District, no work had been taken up in last six to seven years. In Tembli village, the visiting team was told: '*Jyaadatar log gaaon mein bade kaashtkaar ke yahaan kaam karte hai*' (Most people in the village work on the farms of big land owners). These big landowners had around 20–30 acres of land. In another village falling in the same GP (Saalai), field-road construction work had been forcibly stopped, because no measurement of work done was taking place. It was surprising how officials had never noticed till date, and why NREGS work had not been taken up in the last five to six years.

In several villages, a sizeable number of people did not have job cards. A precondition was that only those having an account in the village post office could be engaged in NREGS work. For opening a post office account, the signature of the *Gram Rozagar Sahayak* (GRS) as an introducer/verifier was mandatory. In Dhamangaon, people complained about the Post Master creating problems in opening of account and payment of wages. At several places, it was informed that this was due to the limited amount (₹20,000) that a Branch Post Master could carry, in one transaction. This led to huge delay in payment of wages. This needed to be tackled by the district administration and at the State Post Master General level.

Two critical aspects determined people's availability at the worksite: one was provision of timely employment, when people needed it the most, and the other was payment of wages within a stipulated time. Field experience suggests, these were the weakest features in NREGS implementation. In fact, contractors who engaged workers seeking labour in bonded/debt-bondage labour agreement exploited this weakness to the hilt. They advanced money to persons during the most stressful periods, thereby obligating them to work for them, even if it was on highly exploitative terms. In Ambaadi village (Amravati District), where NREGS work had not been taken up in the last two to three years, villagers told the visiting team how the *thekedaar* (contractor) came and gave advance during June–July when people desperately needed money ('*Khaane ki dikkat hoti hai*' [we were finding it difficult to make provision for daily food], as one said) and took them for work where they were obliged to continue till the contract terms were fulfilled. '*Pakad ke le jaate hain*' (If they try to run away, they are caught and shifted), villagers told the visiting team.

The BDO or officials never tried to dwell on deeper reasons for workers not coming to the worksite when they started the work and dismissed their grievances by saying, 'People are of complaining nature'. In Varajampadi hamlet of Udayapatti GP (Salem District), it was observed that no work was provided during the first four months of the year (January–April), which as villagers pointed out was the period when they needed work/money the most. Here too, like in Thrissur, work even when taken up was of a short duration after which the workers had to migrate in search of work.

In Pithoragarh District (Uttarakhand), despite sufficiency of demand, very few households (in tribal villages) were able to get 100 days of work. Only four cases were recorded (by one of the teams) and that too who were not from the very poor category. There was a considerable demand–supply gap in provision of work, as the average annual availability ranged from 40 to 50 days. Poor SC and tribal women pointed out how they still had to migrate to nearby places along with their little children in search of daily wage work and said it would be ideal if work was available to them in the vicinity of their village. The GPs were resorting to rotation of work, and it was the *Pradhan*'s discretion to allocate the number of days of work to a wage seeker.

Passbooks were not updated in any of the States visited. Only through the job card entry can a labourer and outsider person easily know how many days of work had been provided and how much payment was received. In Nizamabad, job cards had not been updated for years. *In several States, which had Phase I districts, job cards were blank, though the programme was being implemented for the last five years.* The person incharge (*Rozgar Sahayak*) was not filling up the job card. It was surprising how supervisory personnel had missed noticing that not a single entry had been made in the job cards. *Also, entries in job cards and wage amounts in passbook hardly matched and were not complementing each other.*

2.3 WAGE PAYMENT

Wage payments were delayed everywhere, ranging from three weeks to months and even more. Bunching of payments too was noticed in several places. In Ambavaadi (Narmada), payments of two musters (12 days) were pending. There was no way for workers to know when money arrived in their accounts in the post office to enable them to withdraw it. In Dhamangaon, since labourers did not have staying power, invariably they had no choice but to work at other places on lower wages and exploitative terms. Payment problems needed to be sorted out, as on account of non-payment of NREGS work on time, workers were forced to go out of the village wherever work was available.

Payment situation in works undertaken by line departments (such as Forest) was even worse. Here, the delay was a matter of routine than exception. The visiting team was told in Sarguja that (in comparison) 'Vibhagiya (department) *mein* payment *ki stithi aur bhi kharaab hai*' (In the works executed by the departments the position was worse). In Thrissur, a BDO told the visiting team, measurement of agriculture-related works under NREGS had to be approved/signed by the Agriculture officer, which invariably took time, causing at least a month's delay in payment. Officials pointed out to dependence on line department for approval of completed schemes which was the cause behind delay in payment. Wage delay had two important ramifications: it discouraged participation in NREGS works and forced labourers to opt for work for less (but timely paid) wages.

Except for Tamil Nadu (where payment was made in cash), wage payments were routed through the post offices or banks. Experiences of wage seekers as noted in the field suggest that this caused substantial delay in timely payment to beneficiaries though for different reasons. In Rajpur Block of Sarguja, there was one bank for eight to nine GPs. Each had to cover a large number of labourers/wage seekers. As per the local arrangement, the turn of labourers of one/couple of GPs came once in 7–10 days. However, workload of bank officials had also increased manifold on account of such large number of labourers, given their low staff strength.

For instance, Sarguja Kshetriya Gramin Bank had just one manager, one clerk and one peon in its branch in a block. Each branch had to handle 200–300 people. There was just one nationalized bank per block. Banks also faced shortage of cash which got really acute in summer (April, May and June) months. Payment through post offices was quicker. There were four branch post offices in each block and it took around 20 days for a payment to reach. But post offices had a problem of limit in handling of cash.

In several places, it was observed that payment of wages at standard rate was made and uniform measurement recorded which indicated that payment was made irrespective of the work performed. In Dhamoli village (Nalanda District), it was noticed that the wage seekers formed a group of 8–10 members and worked under MGNREGS. Mates were paid ₹10 per day as additional payment for efficiently implementing and monitoring the programme. It was expected that men should generate 80 cft and women 68 cft of work per day to earn their minimum wage of ₹144 under the Act. However, it was found that the single measurement was recorded in the books after completion of works and full wages were paid to every wage seeker who had attended the work. While the workers gained from such an arrangement this showed the laxity in supervision and might have implications for implementation of scheme and quality of work performed as also intra-group equity.

In Mahur Block of Nanded District, out of total 62 GPs, NGOs are implementing the MGNREGS works in 28 GPs. The NGOs are paid 2% of total project expenditure as an honorarium amount. In Shekapur GP, the wages were not paid since September as the GRS has not submitted the muster roll for measurement verification. He was submitting four to five muster rolls at a time. Hence, there was immense delay at the GRS level and Junior Engineer level. The *dalits* and other poor of Mahur Block migrated to Adilabad District as contract labourers for ball picking in cotton fields, brick kilns, timber mill and labour work in construction due to non-availability of work when needed the most, inadequate work and delay in payment.

In Alappuzha District, advance payment after the closing of the muster roll without measurement is one of the good practices which helped in reducing the suffering caused by the delay in payment. The project diary being used by the mates is another good practice that shows the details of the project sanctioned and the milestones in the implementation of the project including the list of equipment used by the labourers and payment of rental charges on equipment to the wage seekers. The diary also provides for workers' comments and observations by the visiting officials.

By and large, the passbooks revealed that whatever be the number of days a labourer worked, work was available/undertaken only during six months in a year and it did not always match the period when they required it most. For remaining months they had to look for work elsewhere. *The need was that sufficient work should be taken up and sequenced in a manner that it was available all through the year* so that people were not forced to migrate and also they had a choice between work available under NREGS and elsewhere.

2.4 PLANNING, IMPLEMENTATION, MONITORING AND MIS

As fund is never a constraint, planning for (1) providing 100 days' employment, and (2) sequencing of works all through the year becomes the most critical aspect of programme implementation. Field experience suggests that the success or failure of NREGS hinges on it.

This aspect of planning is missing. While a fair margin of error, delay and oversight on the part of implementing officials can be excused, repeated instances of lack of planning and poor planning had affected the quality of the programme and its utility for the people. In a tribal village of Gathagaon Block of Keonjhar District, for instance, construction of 40 farm ponds (on individual land) was not only sanctioned during 2008–09, but work was even started on several of them at a time. This led to several distortions such as lack of adequate manpower to work on each pond and workers deserting work in one pond to participate in work on the other pond, or on the pond on their own land. Also, most wage seekers preferred the easy option of initial digging of soft soil in one pond and then conveniently left it mid-way to join work on the other pond where work had just begun. This left work in most of the ponds incomplete.

Of the 40 ponds sanctioned, it took two years to complete seven of them; 16 were not even taken up and 17 were incomplete. Also, the labour budget was inadequate for the sanctioned number of ponds to be completed. It also emerged that several beneficiaries were later not interested in taking up the scheme. The scheme required sequencing or staggered execution.

The concerned line departments are planning and preparing the estimates without any discussion in the GP or community involvement at the village level. There was no discussion at the GS level on the type of schemes being taken up and appropriate execution timing of schemes. Estimates of schemes invariably were based on standard specification and cost norms, leaving no room for local differences sitewise. Hardly any visits were made to collect site-wise measurements, specification, accurate wage cost and manpower and time requirement of works. The sanctioning authorities seemed to be taking up schemes in a routinized manner. This affected the quality of implementation and the asset being constructed.

The Project Director of Keonjhar informed that the rate of completion of schemes in the district was only 3% prior to his joining. As per the records, out of 6,277 works taken up in 2010, only 639 (i.e. 10%) had been completed. Wherever too many schemes were taken up simultaneously without factoring in availability of labour and staff for supervision and implementation, it has led to a larger number of incomplete works.

In Dhalai (Jamirchera GP), it was observed that preparation of work specification and cost estimates did not have any rigour. As a result, schemes were completed and closed without work as per specifications having been executed. There was also no rigour in enforcement of specified work as per estimates which tended to create an impression that inflated estimates of work were being prepared. But completion certification was issued and the labourer was paid full wages without attaining desired work task. This practice which may not be confined to Dhalai but may be getting resorted to elsewhere too fails to get detected because there is no rigorous supervision of schemes and it suits the State (because it can draw larger programme funds) and the workers (who may be getting a full wage without having accomplished requisite work). It is also unfair to the workers and areas where rigorous norms are being observed. This work ethics can affect other development programmes.

The labour budget at the *panchayat* and block levels reflected neither the potential labour demand nor the objective of providing 100 days of assured work to every job card holder who sought work in the village. People across the GPs and States were in desperate need of work and for several wage seekers, particularly for SCs/STs/women, NREGS work was the only dignified option for earning a wage. The officials could provide them with just 30–40 days on an average and much lower in several poorest of pockets (such as Maleghat region of Amravati, and Keonjhar District). Lower labour budget was justified by officials on the ground of incapacity of *panchayat*s to spend the money. But this 'incapacity' was due to inadequate staff, lack of motivation, planning and mobilization—all related to governance and not the lack of demand or need of work. These bottlenecks were not sorted out to enhance the performance in pockets where most vulnerable workers were concentrated.

Another related issue was massive underutilization of NREGS funds, especially in the districts with a larger population of the poor/SCs/STs. For instance, in Keonjhar, in 2010–11, ₹16 crore was the demand placed by one block. An allocation of ₹11.67 crore was made. The amount spent was a meagre ₹1.51 crore (less than 13%). Even in Sarjuga (a Phase I district), where a high expenditure of ₹184 crore (84%) was reported, ₹34 crore went unspent. Additionally, the negative fallout of underutilization was that the budget allocation for next financil year (2011–12) was reduced by ₹6 crore (to ₹212 crore, in comparison to ₹218 crore the previous year).

In Dhalai District, estimates of all schemes taken up under NREGS were for a standard number of days (30) with standard specifications, calculation of labour, man-days and wages. The schemes at different sites could possibly not have had standard width, length, quantum of work and number of days required for their completion. The variety of physical location would not permit it. This implied that uniform quantum of work was being taken up and executed, irrespective of requirement. This would have led either to excess work or insufficient work depending upon the location. This also indicated that the objective seemed to be not so much to plan and execute a scheme efficiently but to generate employment. This would have also led to inflated estimation of work at some places and underestimation at other places. No one seemed to look into it as there was no genuine supervision of scheme.

A substantial opening balance (OB) was being generated every year at the *panchayat* and block levels, as the team observed in Keonjhar. For instance, in Champai GP, the budget for 2010–11 was 15.45 lakh including a huge OB of ₹9.81 lakh. However, the expenditure incurred during the year was less than 50% (₹7.31 lakh) and thereby repeating the pattern for the next financial year (₹8.14 OB for 2011–12). Despite there being a crying need of wage work in the areas and no shortage of money, the officials were not only unable to spend the money but also blatantly said that there was lack of demand.

Instances of State-sponsored community benefit schemes in tribal areas, being abandoned earlier due to some constraints and having the possibility of being resumed under NREGS, were observed. For instance, the team saw a half-completed dry well in a village having scarcity of water. It was taken up some time ago under the Biju Patnaik scheme and the standard budget allocation for it at that time was ₹13,000. However, halfway during implementation, the presence of a large number of stones/rocks made completion difficult within the sanctioned estimate. As there was no scope for getting additional allocation, it was abandoned. The team felt, if there was village-level planning, such incomplete works could have easily been taken up afresh under NREGS and completed on priority basis.

Development of common property resources for employment generation and provision of community benefits were not receiving the attention they deserved due to lack of planning and capacity building. For instance, in Dokseela village, Parvathipuram GP (Vizianagaram), huge tracts of *parambok* land were available which could be developed for social forestry, etc. A water channel too lay derelict and could be revived. Developing public/community assets and making them productive should be the first priority in taking up NREGS works.

In Dhamtari District, payment of ₹8–10 crore for materials was pending across several blocks and *panchayat*s of the district for the past one year because of audit objections. As a result, NREGS works had been halted in several of them. This exposed lack of adequate monitoring for timely intervention. It also showed that field inspections and supervision were lacking. If inspections had been undertaken, these were evidently poor in quality for not having addressed such issues.

While planning for NREGS works it had to be kept in mind that work had not only to be spread across the year, but also be made available to those in utmost need of it. *Planning for employment had to be done in a manner that work was available when there was maximum demand for it.* This is usually when *rabi* harvesting is over and before the rains start, and further when *kharif* sowing is over. Neither the planning nor execution of work synchronized with this requirement.

The technical feasibility of schemes and supervision of work under execution were, in general, unsatisfactory. Field visits suggested that either the professional competence of staff engaged was inadequate or the officials were simply interested in providing employment but were indifferent to quality of implementation. For instance, a drain/water channel in Dhalai District was constructed in a manner that seepage caused by it was eroding the boundary of nearby houses and fields. Similarly, the slope and turn of a road under construction had the potential of causing landslide. This called for identification of design and execution flaws in various schemes and training of technical staff about them and rigorous supervision of schemes by senior officials.

In some tribal pockets (e.g. Dhalai District), because of desperate need for survival due to lack of livelihood opportunities and non-provision of NREGS work, people were engaged in collecting/ cutting fuel wood banned by the forest department, for sale in the market. There was a need to provide such people livelihood under NREGS which would save the forests from degradation.

In Kunbat village (Ningat GP) of Narmada District, out of 19 community wells executed, nine remained incomplete because the department neither provided material (bricks, sand, cement) nor released payments in time. The beneficiaries had to take loans (about ₹44,000) to buy materials. Because of rains, some of the freshly dug wells collapsed, causing not only wastage of material purchased but also indebtedness of tribals. The government had transferred the risk to the tribals and had created conditions wherein the beneficiary was forced to take loans to save his asset. This reflected not only lack of planning but also timely intervention to protect the incomplete works and farmers' interests. Planning for NREGS also failed to target the vulnerable population and prevent ecological degradation so as to achieve the twin objective of providing work as well as restoring the environment harmoniously.

In the *Chara Vikas Yojana* (fodder development programme) undertaken on a large scale in Pithoragarh District, three vital things were missing: (a) preference for traditional fodder species (suitable for local ecology and cattle), (b) undertaking an assessment of the long-term ecological ramifications of cultivating species of the plains (Napier grass, MP *chari*, oat) on a mass scale and their suitability in terms of nutrition content, soil, climate, altitude and local livestock and (c) failure to involve *van panchayat*s for growing green fodder on their land which would have led to the development of *panchayat* assets and participation of people in its planning and execution of wage programme.

In Thrissur, Dhalai and Pithoragarh, no norms of work were laid down for payment. There was no piece rate prescribed for actual output of work. Daily attendance (twice in a day, in case of Thrissur) was required to earn a day's wages.

All in all, poor planning meant several things: low utilization of funds, inadequate provisioning of labour budget, parking of funds, several schemes not getting started, poor completion rate and work done (incomplete) becoming infructuous.

While a good deal of data was being generated in the MIS, it was not being: (1) shared at the *panchayat/* GS level, and (2) discussed or analyzed by the programme staff so as to improve implementation of NREGS. Salem District had generated unique data, whereby a break-up of man-days of work by each social category households (i.e. caste-wise: SC/ST/ OBC/General) registered under NREGS was shown against the number of total households in that village. However, the data which pointed out to large-scale exclusion of SCs/STs (as they were not given job cards) and getting less employment than OBC and General category groups sadly was not taken note of for corrective intervention by officials.

In some places, the entry in the MIS was not reliable. For instance, in Nizamabad District, the number of household categories into SCs, STs, OBCs and General was inaccurate. In several places, while the NREGS registration was based on recent registration of households, information about the total number of households was based on the last census (2001) data. This created avoidable confusion. In some places (say like Khandaballur in Nizamabad District), cumulative number of days worked by an individual was incorrectly recorded in that it included work done in the previous year as well. There was a real possibility of such incorrect data entered elsewhere too.

In Dhamtari, software for tracking the movement of muster roll to determine the delay in processing, measurement, completion and payment was introduced by the District Magistrate. A register was maintained at the district level for this purpose. Still there was huge delay in submission and verification of muster roll which the software system could not detect. Nearly 17 GRS had been dismissed for delay in submission of muster roll. Around three BDOs had been penalized to pay a fine of ₹1,000 for the delay.

Social audit is an important tool for stock-taking of NREGS work, ensuring accountability of implementing officials and hearing grievances of people. Andhra Pradesh was the only State among those inspected by the visiting team, where the exercise was regular and fairly independent, leading to detection of anomalies and subsequent action by the government. There was a full-fledged Directorate for it. While it was a government-led effort and bureaucratic in nature, officials claimed that it was conducted autonomously. There were non-government functionaries on its panel. A non-official headed it and the Commissioner had no control over this functionary. Government functionaries such as the PD participated in its district-level exercise. About

₹18 crore worth of misappropriation had been detected and action taken (including dismissal, recovery of money) against the erring officials. Another instance come across was in Chelakarra GP of Thrissur District where the team was informed about social audit being organized twice a year. However, no complaint was registered. No other district visited by the committee had carried out social audit as prescribed.

2.5 EQUITY ISSUES

The issue of equity in the implementation of NREGS is important to see whether the programme benefits are being reasonably shared by all workers/households registered for work or in need of it, in a given unit of implementation. Regrettably, this aspect is overlooked by the programme officials.

The most striking example of it was lower levels of employment, lesser number of man-days generated, work not taken up in areas which had concentration of SCs/STs, higher levels of poverty, malnutrition, migration and landlessness. There was no effort to target these areas and specifically monitor performance of NREGS in these locations.

In Andaman Island, most of the workers in NREGS were tribals (from Chota Nagpur region of Jharkhand) and SCs (from West Bengal and other regions). They faced double disadvantage of not having productive assets (since they neither have land, nor land has been allocated by the government) and not being recognized as *adivasi*s or from SCs.

As a result, they are neither targeted under NREGS, nor affirmative programmes under Category IV taken up for them. For instance, in Ferrargunj Block, out of 10,954 households, job cards had been issued to 7,645 persons of which only less than one-fourths (1,797 persons) had been provided employment. Overall, nearly 65% of the population in the district is landless, a sizable part of which would be in need of NREGS work. No planning had been done to target this population.

In many GPs of Nizamabad District, a highly unusual phenomenon was observed, that is, of less than 50% of SC job card holders reporting for work and, more importantly, SC job card holders having worked for lesser number of days than those of General and backward caste (BC) categories. In one of the villages of Bichkunda *mandal*, the average number of days worked by General category workers was 20, while it was 10 days for SCs. In Achapalli, where there were 400 households, less than 50% of SCs participated in NREGS and

the man-days generated by BCs/other workers was double (941) compared to SC workers. This dimension of NREGS implementation was neither taken note of at the district level nor at the State level. This skewed participation is striking since Andhra Pradesh allows more than 100 days of work for people from SC and ST categories.

There was no evidence that there were better avenues of employment available to SCs which could have affected their lower participation in NREGS. In fact, as per records in the *mandal* office, 30% of SCs and 40% of total NREGS workers were not reporting for work in an area which is among the most backward and has a large number of landless households. The agrarian structure of the area provided the possible explanation. As discussions in Madnoor and Kutcher Blocks revealed, the area is dominated by powerful landed farmers from Reddy community who use SCs/STs as attached (bonded) labourers on their fields (the practice is known as *jeetam*).

Another dimension of social exclusion was the large-scale omission of *dalit*s in the distribution of MGNREGS job cards in Salem District of Tamil Nadu. There was a substantial difference—in the range of 20% to 40%—between the number of SC households and the job cards issued. This exclusion of areas especially where there was concentration of SCs, STs and other poor was disturbing. This was striking in Omalur Block. For instance, in an SC colony of Balbaki village, job cards had not been issued to 50% of the families. In Talaichola GP, out of 1,300 families, 650 (40%) were not registered for NREGS. These left-out persons were not allowed to participate in NREGS work. Officials made the visiting team believe that the landless and poor of the SC *basti* had not come forth to apply for job cards. This insensitive attitude of officials is unacceptable. It was required of them to reach out to these sections of workers as they were in need of work the most given their asset-lessness and poverty. A job card should have been issued to SC/ST households straightaway. One among the plausible reasons for SCs/STs not getting registered could be the pressure exerted by landholders.

In Thrissur District, job cards had been slashed by 70%. This included SCs and STs. In Geechad village (Junamoda GP) in Narmada (Phase I district), out of 145 households, only 102 had job cards. Issuing to the rest was under process as the visiting team was told, despite the fact that the programme was in execution here for six years.

Instances of SC families being denied NREGS job cards were observed in Chithyal GP in Tadur *mandal* and Jakarpally *mandal* of Nizamabad; Basanpur GP in Keonjhar and in Coimbatore District.

In Narmada District, where little work under NREGS was initiated, it was alleged that officials and NREGS staff were not taking up work so as to allow *kapaas* (cotton) farmers' easy and cheap availability of labour (at ₹60 per day). In fact, as some said, if the Patels (landed farmers) did not give them advance as loan for consumption, they would face starvation. This system of advance payment to the labourers is the foundation of bonded labour system which binds them to work on wages dictated by the employer. The entire system of advance payment to labourers by big farmers and the labourers being taken away to far-off places for work is well known. Officials were just not sensitive to this brazen exploitation and continued to argue that people were not reporting for NREGS work and therefore there was no demand for work.

In Talaichola GP of Salem, where India's biggest and well-known coffee estates are located, NREGS work was being taken up only during the four months from April to July and the average number of days that people were able to get work here was 40. While officials said that workers preferred work at coffee estates as wages were higher, discussions with villagers indicated they were happier to do NREGS work round the year and would prefer it to the work at coffee estates. It therefore seemed that the work was not being taken up to allow the estates access to cheap labour. In Seethanagaram *mandal* (Vizianagaram District), conversations with NREGS workers in one village (Khasapeta) indicated that the credit-linked bonded work agreement was widely prevalent in the area. Around 50–60 persons from the village had gone out to work in nearby villages/places as they had taken ₹5,000 advance loan from the contractor.

In Chinna Kodagu (Vizianagram District), no work had been taken up during the last two years. In another adjacent village (Burnapore, Dharmara), people openly complained of 'caste bias', alleging that NREGS works were provided only to workers of the BC community while SCs had deliberately been kept out of work for the past two years. In a clear instance of violation of NREGS norms, only workers from the BC community were assigned work undertaken on an SC person's land. The beneficiary and workers from other communities were kept out. This obviously seemed a caste bias by the *sarpanch* which remained undetected by officials.

In an ST colony in Barlam (Nizamabad District) which had around seven SSS groups, residents complained about social exclusion of their *tandaa* (habitation) despite repeated requests to start the work. Work had not been taken up in their colony for the last three years and no mate was chosen from their colony.

The nexus between local officials and land owners is usually responsible for not taking up work when the poor desperately needed it. An elderly woman, in one of the meetings, was bold enough to raise her voice against officials while other people remained tongue-tied. She complained that NREGS work was deliberately stopped just two days after it had begun, ostensibly under the pressure of big farmers. People also complained of delay in wage payment by the branch post office, low realization of wages (ranging from ₹30 to ₹60) on account of difficult work, stringent SoR and mates/staff colluding with farmers in not taking up work.

In Kamarpara, a habitation of 14 households of the Kamars (STs) adjacent to the reserve forest area and whose residents are among the poorest people in Dhamtari District, the visiting team encountered the abject poverty and utter helpless situation they were in. While they had job cards, the forest department had just not engaged them in its works or allowed NREGS work to be taken up in their *para* (habitation) for the past several years. The GP did not keep them informed about work to be started in other *para*s of the area or date and time of taking up allocated work in their *para*. The *panch* and *sarpanch* of the GP asked them to go back when they went to them for seeking for work ('*Panchayat waale bataate nahin hain; Waapis kar dete hain, panch, sarpanch*' [*Panchayat* people do not inform us; rather, *panch* and *sarpanch* tell us to go back]). Their land *patta* applications were also pending with the forest department. However, for the past five months, they had been able to get some work.

Work was not being equitably generated in all blocks, *panchayat*s and habitations within them. In Keonjhar District, the ward member of one *palli* (habitation) *sabha* complained how his voice remained unheard in GS meetings. In interior and hilly tribal areas, since several habitations of one village were located far apart from each other, several of them had non-allocation of work in their areas. Also, it was important that work was available within 2–3 km so that people could avail of the opportunity. Work taken up in a distant location deprived them of the opportunity to participate. The most common complaint was concentration in one location/habitation—usually the headquarter village of the GP or the village to which the *sarpanch* belonged or in villages/GP where dominant castes were in majority. As we saw in Salem District (Tamil Nadu), in GPs dominated by Vanniyars (most backward caste, MBC), residents' level of awareness and collective articulation were high. They were more active and assertive, in contrast to adjacent *panchayats* (having SCs and STs in majority). In Ediapatti GP for instance, where MBCs were dominant social groups, not only was its labour budget high, but also it ensured that 100 days of work was available to workers. In fact, they demanded another 50 days of work. Also, they were drawing the full stipulated wages of ₹130. Last year, out of 385 households, 120 families completed 100 days of work here. This was not so in SC/ST-dominated *panchayats*. In Dhalai District (Tripura), it was observed that GPs in vicinity of the town/block headquarters had a higher labour budget and expenditure in comparison to the GPs in remote areas.

In Mahuli Jahangi GP of Amravati District, where landlessness was as high as 78%, during 2008–09 farm ponds were dug on landowners' land (belonging to OBC category) which is against the NREGS guidelines. *In Maharashtra, there is still confusion and old EGS norms which are no longer valid (as the one above) are being followed in NREGS implementation.* Even in Dhalai District, as seen in Jagganathpur GP, farm ponds were sanctioned to better-off tribal households while poor tribal households were neglected. In the same GP, instance of APL households getting subsidies under NREGS affirmative programme was also observed. There was some degree of collusion and corruption in the way disproportionate benefits were being extended to the better-off households. In Amravati, it was also observed that SC/ST lands were not taken up for development. In Nalanda, lands of SCs were not taken up under Category IV works.

Inequity, though unintended, can emerge from State policy as well. In Tamil Nadu, till last year the policy was against taking up affirmative action (Category IV) works. This tended to deprive SCs/STs of the entitled benefits which they were getting in other States. The Tamil Nadu Government had also directed that in a *panchayat*, only one scheme could be taken up at a time. The location factor determined who would participate in work. Several schemes were being implemented at a considerable distance from habitations in a *panchayat* which discouraged participation on account of inconvenience, lack of connectivity, cost and time factors. As a woman worker in Salem District told the visiting team, when work got transferred to the other habitation, she could not go as it was more than 10 km away and the auto fare of reaching the destination was ₹20. The shelf of works was limited to only

earthen works, and having no material component. Construction work was also barred. Hence, State's directive was itself preventing people from getting 100 days of work and non-availability of work in their vicinity.

In Pithoragarh District, largely because of the single-minded focus in terms of allocation of resources and attention on *Chara Vikas Yojana* under NREGS, the shelf of works undertaken was limited and included construction of canals (*nahar*), check dams, check walls, compost pits, ponds, etc. Here too, beneficiary-oriented Category IV works were virtually non-existent. At several places, the poor residents stressed on the urgent need for building small water storage structures for irrigation, land levelling (to make land cultivable) and taking up micro watershed development structures for harvesting rainwater, melting snow etc. and land development activities on private land which would not only allow the most efficient use of small agricultural land holdings but turn unutilized land into productive assets.

Actual wage realization against the work accomplished was another area which threw up equity issues. Sadly, wage realization was very low against the work done, especially in the tribal pockets of Tamil Nadu, Maharashtra and Andhra Pradesh. In Udaypati GP of Salem District, it was learnt that the average wage realization was ₹80, while ₹95 was the maximum, as against the prescribed rate of ₹130 (last year). In Sadrabadi GP of Amravati District, where the average wage was ₹105, actual wage realization was in the range of ₹70–80. Wherever this low wage realization was accompanied by hard soil work (say in rocky areas), or delay in wage payment, the labourers opted out of NREGS work. In Vizianagaram District, women workers complained of getting ₹70–80 for a day's labour saying, '*Jitna kaam kartein hain utna nahin milta*' (We do not get as much wages as the work we do). However, officials contested it by saying this was because they put in only four to five hours of work. Here and in other States, there was considerable gap in work performed between work as assessed by officials and as perceived by labourers. The problem lies in delayed measurement by officials in the absence of workers.

Another dimension of intra-group inequity was that time spent on lead and lift was creating wage differentials. In Seethanagaram *mandal* (Vizianagaram District), women of some SSS groups engaged on work in the desilting of a huge waterbody/MI tank complained that wage realization for groups which had been assigned work farther from the bund was far lower. They had to dig, carry and deposit the soil on the bund. This resulted in as ₹30–40 wage difference. If groups were allowed to deposit the excavated soil nearby just like a heap, then the lead would be reduced, time and effort saved and wages would increase.

In Dhamtari District, the visiting team got the information that masons (skilled category of workers) were not only drawing the prevailing market-rate wages which were higher than stipulated under NREGS but also working for 200 days. Their wages were being booked under material component and therefore did not attract notice. In Coimbatore also, instances of workers having worked more than 100 days were observed in Vellamadai village in Sarcarsamakulam Block. In Amravati, instances of workers who had been paid for more than 127 days of work were noticed. In fact, an instance of one person working for almost a year and receiving payment through other people's accounts was also observed.

In Sarguja District, in order to ensure equity in the distribution of subsidy in affirmative works, the incumbent Collector had put a financial limit for schemes of individual land development while his predecessor had taken measures to disallow bigger farmers/landowners getting the benefit of the private pond scheme under NREGS. However, how a standardized norm to ensure equity could lead to distortions/unintended consequences was observed in Paadhi GP of Balrampur Block in the same district. Sadhuram, an SC, who worked for 103 days under NREGS, desperately needed well (an entitlement under NREGS) to cultivate his land productively. However, the eligibility guidelines of the district permitted it only to those having five or less acres of land. While he had 10 acres of land, six acres of it was *taand* (distributed in small, barren plots lying uncultivated). He, therefore, sold a small portion of his land to his sister and used the money to construct a well next to his house. Also, the eligibility for land development was up to two hectares of land. Some of the *adivasi*s had land more than two hectares, though most of it was uncultivable. They sold part of their land to become eligible for the land development scheme. In fact, in this village, tribals with 10 acres of land and tribals who were landless had both worked for 100-plus days pointing out to the urgent need of work irrespective of land ownership. Land acreage/ownership, without looking into the quality of land, cannot be a sole criterion of assessing poverty and need in such destitute tribal areas.

In Dinkara GP of the same district, while *patta*s had been given to landless SCs and STs, this was not followed up by identification of plots and marking the boundaries. The beneficiaries did not therefore know the *chauhaddi* (boundary wall) of their plot. Such people were deprived of the benefit of affirmative action programmes especially relating to land development that was being taken up in the district, due to the inaction of revenue department officials. Other officials (from NREGS, forest department) too did not think of taking help of revenue officials to mark boundaries and then take up land development. This was exclusion resulting from lack of convergence.

Among the 19 districts—especially those having a sizable tribal population, or which were Phase I NREGS districts—the incidence of landlessness was very high among SCs and STs, for instance, in tribal/SC pockets of Narmada, Sarguja, Amravati, Keonjhar and Dhalai districts. These persons should have been the obvious targets for NREGS. However, nowhere did the visiting team find the targeting of such people/pockets for provisioning 100 days of employment. Rather, the overall number of person-days of work was lower here in comparison to other areas. On the other hand, many persons who were not landless were able to complete 100 days. They may also be equally needy. But what is being stressed is the need for focussing on landless, particularly the SCs/STs who are most vulnerable and have to migrate in search of work if local employment is not available.

A good example of State-led affirmative action was brought to the visiting team's attention in Vizianagaram. In Andhra Pradesh, SC and ST job card holders can avail of more than 100 days of work in areas affected by drought. The additional funds required for this purpose come from State budget. In the last two months of the financial year 2011–12, the State was concentrating on SC and ST households for affirmative action programmes such as providing wage labour, as the visiting team was told. During 2010–11, average number of days of work done by an SC worker was 83 days while for the ST worker it was 78 in Andhra Pradesh. The team was also informed that the State directive was to give preference to SC, ST and landless workers in the opening of all NREGS work. SSS groups had the total freedom to organize employment for 100 days for their groups, implying that availability of work was not dependent on demand registered. Together, SC (10.5%) and ST (9.5%) categories constituted 20% of the district's population. Since many of them are landless, and those with land have very small holdings, they are most dependent on NREGS work for livelihood. Yet, by and large, the visiting team did not come across beneficiaries availing of the generous provision of work, thereby losing a rare opportunity of improving their economic condition.

Overall, equity aspect was taken much better care of in Viziangaram District (and to some extent in Sarguja District) than anywhere else. Andhra Pradesh also led in affirmative action for the persons with disability. In Paidapondapalli GP for instance, there were separate SSS for disabled workers. Such workers were not only participating in NREGS work with other groups but also given 30% extra allowance in their wages. Also, during summer season, when working in the scorching sun is energy sapping, an extra allowance is permitted. Similarly, in drought-prone areas, higher wages for NREGS work had been allowed.

The SSS system in Andhra Pradesh and provision of an SC/ST promoter in Kerala had helped in mobilizing labourers and people from disadvantaged groups for NREGS work. The SSS system had broken the stranglehold of FAs by neutralizing their power and bogus mustering. However, it was not uniformly successful. For instance, while in Vizianagaram District it had improved NREGS performance, it had made no dent in Nizamabad District where NREGS work was abysmally low and exclusion of marginalized glaring.

In Narmada District, in villages located in forest areas, NREGS funds were being used to take up schemes as construction of rubber wall and *nala* bunding for soil and moisture conservation and creating water-spots for wild animals/birds, which only provided wage employment. *Panchayat* was not authorized to take up any work, only the forest department could. Hence, people were not only deprived of NREGS work but also the work undertaken was of little benefit to them.

In Pithoragarh District, where large-scale cultivation of fodder had been taken up on the government land with NREGS funds, its distributive aspect was skewed in several ways: (1) There was no equitable system of distribution of the free-of-cost fodder harvested. It was based on the number of milch cattle holdings of households. As a result, people with a larger number of livestock got the major share while those not having cattle were deprived of any share in the collective resource generated from public investment. (2) While members of a poor family worked as wage-labour, well-off families could obtain fodder-harvest without/minimal labour contribution or cost. (3) While it was meant to be shared by people of all nearby habitations (typically a village had two to four habitations or *tog*), only residents of the *tog* where the plot for fodder cultivation was located

were able to reap the harvest due to the proximity of location and access to information. Hence, there is not enough fodder for all. (4) In no place was an SHG distributing the fodder, as claimed by the PD. By and large, it appeared to be the *Pradhan*'s discretion. The harvest is made on first-cum-first-serve basis, with no pre-determined norms for setting a time and date for harvest known to all. The *Pradhan* announces the time of harvest with a message being sent out to the villagers. (5) Utilization of government resources for collective benefit has to factor in needs, demands and priorities of different sections of society so that distribution of benefits is equitably spread. This certainly did not happen in planning and management of the scheme. It was indeed diverting the benefits from common land to a small section of people. It had become a State-sponsored free fodder provision scheme for relatively better-off people.

Convergence can also be a conduit for providing subsidy to big farmers/landholders and others. In Edavaialgu GP (Thrissur District), it was brought to the visiting team's notice that APL families too were getting registered for NREGS job cards to take advantage of the scheme for preparing fields for vegetable cultivation. Under the scheme, digging work and bed preparation for vegetable cultivation could be taken up from NREGS funds. The agriculture department was providing the seeds. This reduced the cost of cultivation. Dubious instances of convergence in the same district were of NREGS labour working on veterinary farm land for growing fodder and Kudumbshree groups leasing land and using NREGS fund for vegetable cultivation.

In the tribal district of Dhalai (Tripura), there was an overloading of subsidy (i.e. the same person being a beneficiary for different schemes). In fact, NREGS funds were being routed to different line departments who selected their beneficiaries under their departmental scheme. The most resourceful persons managed to corner these benefits. For instance, a person who has been sanctioned a scheme for a check dam or a *lunga* on his land for irrigation under NREGS was additionally given fish-seeds and fish-feed under composite fish culture scheme of the fisheries department. Beneficiaries who were given land development schemes were also given scheme for horticultural plantation. If this convergence had taken place through different funding sources and schematic provisions, it could have been justified. But in Dhalai, such departmental schemes were using NREGS funds.

In the same district, under Category IV works (affirmative action), almost a hill had been broken to level a large tract of land owned by a tribal (retired soldier). It was learnt that the plot was more than the beneficiary's capacity to utilize it. For this work, nearly ₹4.25 lakh of NREGS funds were spent. There was a need to have an optimum limit of subsidy and the scale of work (limit to land levelling, in this case) that could be undertaken for individual beneficiaries in order that scarce resources were better distributed among needy persons. The need was to select a large number of people for such benefits rather than benefits being cornered by one or two influential persons whether tribal or non-tribal. The distributive aspect of the programme appeared very skewed.

2.6 GOVERNANCE AND STAFF-RELATED ISSUES

In Madnoor Mandal of Nizamabad District, across several GPs the visiting team heard of pending payments that were due for the last two-and-a-half years. This area in Telengana region is among the interior-most parts of the district and is drought prone. People showed the officers bunch of NREGS slips—unpaid wages that were still due to them. There was discontent and anger against the *Mandal* Programme Development Officer (MPDO) and other NREGS officials who had not attended to their complaints despite several representations to their office by the people.

The reasons were manifold: discrepancies (such as double job cards of individual beneficiary) that had been detected in social audit, pending payments with the post office on account of incorrect names/job card numbers on the wage slips, pending biometric verification of beneficiaries, lack of staff (field functionaries in particular), short duration of posting of officials, etc. As the entire process of data entry and decision making was computerized (based in Hyderabad), it had made matters worse as local officials were handicapped in providing immediate relief at their level. In fact, this technological intervention had eroded the entire democratic process in NREGS.

Obviously, the poor would not come for work if they did not get their wages in time. Because of widespread resentment on this account, others too were discouraged to come for work. As a result, no NREGS work had been taken up for almost two years in several GPs. Since there was a long history to this problem and local officials such as APO, MPDO and FPO have not had a long and continuous stint in the district, it needed to be monitored at the district level. The District Programme Officer should

have got in touch with officials in Hyderabad (State capital) for quick redress of the problem which had not happened.

Shortage of NREGS-related staff and overloading of work in particular officials was one of the factors responsible for poor implementation of the programme. In Maleghat, a tribal region in Amravati, one GRS was looking after two to three *panchayat*s whereas norms specify one. In Saalai GP, having an account in the post office was a compulsory precondition for participation in NREGS work. And for opening such an account, one had to get the signatures of the GRS as an introducer/verifier. 'It took me seven days to locate the GRS', a villager told the visiting team. As a result, there was heavy demand on lower officials especially in case of dual charge which led to irregularity in opening of offices and attending to programme matters. Most of the time, the GRS was not available in his office.

Even after 20 months of joining, the newly recruited batch of BDOs in Amravati had not received any training. As a result, they had no knowledge or exposure to NREGS. One BDO confessed that he was implementing the scheme by consulting the scheme manual and reading the circulars. He did not have clarity on many issues. The *Tehsildar* also complained that as no training had taken place, they had no idea of maintenance of records and how and what to inspect in records. There was no extension officer in several blocks and a general shortage of technical officers in engineering and agriculture departments. Also, distances between villages and GPs in this hilly region were long, which led to inconvenience and greater travel cost. Public transport was infrequent. No transport allowance was given to staff (who travelled on motorcycles). Phone connectivity was poor, leading to fewer field visits. Most of the staff were outsiders to the area and considered posting in the area as a punishment. '*Tribal* areas *mein baahar ka aadmi thahartaa nahin, taluka mein rehtaa hai*', an official posted here told the visiting team (In tribal areas, outside employees do not stay in the place of their posting but reside in the *taluka/* headquarters and commute from there for work). All these had led to general neglect of the area and the people harboured 'immense negative feeling towards the administration' in Maleghat.

In Pithoragarh District, there was an acute shortage of BDOs (as many as 68% posts were lying vacant, the visiting team was informed) and the programme was literally being run by the *Gram Vikas Adhikari*. In Thrissur, during the visiting team's interactions with Panacherry GP officials, it learnt that there were only two staff members per GP for all NREGS activities. GPs were dependant on line department officials for preparation, approval and closure of schemes after completion. For example, for schemes related to land development, the Agriculture Officer was the key functionary. This caused delays in implementation.

In Keonjhar District, higher officials restricted their visits to the block *panchayat* and GP offices and hardly visited programme sites or met beneficiaries in the village. This may be happening in other States as well. It is also learnt that the BDO who is the key official for implementing the NREGS does not keep record of landless persons, which is maintained by/kept at *Tehsildar*'s office. They have data only of *pattas* allocated by the forest department. There is no coordination between the two. As a result, landless persons fail to get focus in provisioning of NREGS works.

In Mahur Block of Nanded, MGNREGS works were being simultaneously executed by the GP, forest department, agriculture department and minor irrigation department, independent of each other, without any coordination. At each worksite, hardly 20–40 wage seekers were found. The funds are transferred at the district level to the concerned line departments. It would be advisable for the Block Programme Officer to coordinate with line departments so that different MGNREGS works are well-spread across the year, and properly lined and sequenced.

While workers' demand for work was hardly registered in most of the States, in Bagmara Panchayat of Dhalai District (Tripura) and other places too, a 100% provision of work as per demand, not realizing that in the employment vis-à-vis demand was uniformly maintained in records. The total number of households demanding work and the total number of households provided NREGS work tallied in toto. Real demand was never shown on record and in the demand shown, it was the number of days of work actually provided by the State. This meant that (a) officials were underplaying work actually demanded, and (b) overplaying people's provision of work—in best of circumstances people could be absenting themselves from work. That this has never attracted the attention of senior officials is reflective of lack of intervention for improving the quality of implementation, integrity of data collection and entry, field inspections and cross checking of records with social reality on the ground.

Technical support to the NREGS programme in several places visited was inadequate. This impacted the quality of schemes. The level of technical competence of staff sanctioning land and water-related schemes was low. Competence of engineers left a lot to be desired and inspection by officials was superficial.

For all NREGS schemes implemented by any agency, including various line departments (such as Forest, Irrigation and Horticulture), the need was to make the *panchayat* as the focal point. The processes of decentralization and democratization were very important. While line departments had the right to prepare estimates, the timing of initiating work should not be decided by them but by the *panchayat* so that the labourers are informed in advance and their availability ensured. All records pertaining to work such as estimates, man-days to be generated, etc. needed to be with the *panchayat* so that not only people knew details about work, but *panchayat*s were facilitated to monitor the programme and carry out social audits. Once a scheme was prepared and sanctioned, line departments should have a meeting with the GP to share details and request for mobilizing labour. At the moment, budget and expenditure details of NREGS work were prepared and submitted by the respective line departments by the District Programme Officer. They were not submitting muster rolls, work sanction order to blocks or *panchayat*s nor was their counter-signature obtained. The entire process was centralized as the money was directly transferred to the line department, without keeping the block or *panchayat* in the loop.

Mobilization of labour was very weak—Thrissur (Kerala) and Vizianagaram (Andhra Pradesh) districts being the only exceptions where there were SC/ST promoters/SSS groups, respectively. This prevented landless and SCs/STs from demanding work and participating in it. Considering that caste and class bias played their role in provision or work and nexus between local officials and landed farmers influenced the opening of works, there was an urgent need of a functionary to mobilize labour, particularly from SCs/STs and landless poor.

In Pithoragarh District (Uttarakhand), a large-scale experimentation of fodder cultivation on civil-soyam (government revenue) land had been taken up. Species such as Oat (*jaee*) MP chari, Napier grass, etc. were being cultivated in two to five hectare-size fenced plots. Labour work and material cost (seeds, maintenance, etc.) were being booked under NREGS. However, this precious produce was being harvested free of cost by few villagers (only those having milch cattle) without any revenue being paid to the government. No norms for sharing the fodder among households were laid down or any record maintained on its production and distribution. Civil-soyam land is generally used for building societal infrastructure and has competing uses.

Diverting its use for cultivating fodder on a large scale by the district was possibly a case of violation of State Revenue Law. Legally, only the State Government has the power to divert its uses. Also, in some blocks, the selection of the sites was disputed (SCs/STs claimed in some places that the land had been, in principle, allocated to them as *patta*s, but formal papers had yet not been given).

In Amravati District (Maharashtra), the EGS format was still being used for NREGS. The government machinery, it seemed, had not discontinued the earlier EGS framework and the transition to NREGS had not taken place. Accordingly, while affirmative action for landless did not have their priority, labourers were being employed on rich farmers' fields for agriculture and plantation works and ponds given to landed farmers from the OBC. In Rasgaon GP, only one work was undertaken and that too on the field of a non-BPL, OBC farmer who was the *sarpanch*. Plantation on non-SC/ST land is not allowed under NREGS (but was apparently permissible under the EGS). The Maharashtra Government also included farmers under the loan waiver scheme as beneficiary of individual land development under NREGS.

In Dhamtari, a Phase I district, across several villages of different blocks and *panchayat*s, job cards had been taken away by officials since June 2011 under the pretext of renewal. Villagers hence could not demand work.

In Amravati, 30% additional wages for physically challenged workers was not being paid and was a violation of the NREGA.

Job cards were not being issued in continuous serial numbers as observed in Chidgiri GP of Nanded.

The quality of record keeping was poor, especially in Amravati and Nalanda Districts. In several districts, complaint registers were mostly blank at district, block and GP levels. In Dhalai, asset register, cashbook and employment registers were not found to be updated. Same was the case with job cards. In Narmada, instances of *kachha* muster rolls were noticed while in Amravati, muster rolls not being in the GP office but in the house of *Gram Sevak* were observed. In Keonjhar, vouchers without signatures and date were found. In Pithoragarh, discrepancies such as missing muster rolls, incomplete job card entries and absence of photographs were observed.

2.7 QUALITY OF WORKS

At several places across States, it was observed that construction works allowed under the ambit of NREGS, such as wells, ponds (both digging of new ones and desilting), check dams and roads suffered from technical flaws or lack of supervision by engineers/officials of line departments. In a large number of cases, earth-related works were taken up shortly before the onset of monsoon and therefore were not completed before it arrived. Much of this work would be washed away during the rains and go waste. In some cases, it may lead to inordinate delay in completion as water would get accumulated in them.

There were instances of (1) incomplete and (2) technically unsound works which are shown as completed, approved and closed in office records (as confirmed by officials). There was no system in place to monitor the quality of assets and people's satisfaction in respect of it. Since participation in the GS is weak, the issue does not come up in official discourse. Social audit system has not taken up. This results in lack of accountability. In Gathagaon Block of Keonjhar, one of the four sides of a useful community pond had been breached by rainwater due to a simple flaw in design: the outlet being in the wrong place. In another instance in a tribal village, there was no causeway near a 2-km road and its slope had not been properly made. There was a real possibility of the rains splitting the road. Ironically, this happened in Keonjhar where, inappropriately, not only were engineers the driving force behind NREGS implementation (the Junior Engineer was the nodal officer for implementation at the *panchayat* level), other NREGS staff such as the Programme Officer appeared to be completely rely on him in such matters.

In Maleghat (Amravati District), the proposed compacting (*murum* blanketing) by the Public Works Department (PWD) of nearly 40 roads constructed under NREGS were lying incomplete, thereby causing asset degeneration. Estimates of skill/material component of work had been prepared nearly eight months ago (March–April 2011) but work had not been executed, as private contractors were not willing to undertake work on rates being offered by the government. The issue had not been resolved leading to the possibility of the earthen work on these roads going waste.

2.8 LAND DEVELOPMENT

Land development was an important work undertaken under NREGS across the States. This provision had particular importance because *patta*s had been given to tribals and other forest dwellers under the Forest Rights Act (FRA) in some of the States visited. NREGS funds were used by the district administration in developing this land to make it cultivable. The scheme also benefitted those whose land, because of widespread degradation on account of natural factors, had ceased to be cultivable. This provision restores ecological stability. For instance, in the case of Andaman and Nicobar Islands where a great deal of scarce agricultural land had become saline because of ingress of sea water during the tsunami disaster, a proper use of this programme along with other technical inputs can restore the soil. This activity could be taken up under affirmative action (Category IV schemes).

There was a huge demand for land development among eligible beneficiaries (largely STs) in the States visited.

The use of NREGS for this activity had led to increased areas under cultivation as was claimed in Dediyapada and Sagebara Blocks of Narmada District.

In Nalanda District, no works under Category IV was being executed as very few SCs have land and land in possession of BPL, small and marginal farmers is cultivable. But these groups have benefitted from *Ahar* and *Pyne* irrigation water storage structures surrounding their cultivable areas (*khand*) which were desilted under NREGS. The water table has increased by 40–50 feet in plains and by 20 feet in hilly terrain, as claimed by officials. Due to rejuvenation of *Ahar* and *Pyne* systems, the district administration could save ₹10 crore which was spent towards the diesel subsidy for harvesting underground water, as informed. The block administration had distributed three cents of land to the SC landless households for homestead purposes. Part of this land could be used for backyard vegetable cultivation/horticulture.

In some places, land development works were a misnomer for agricultural work of ineligible farmers. In Thrissur, for example, land development works involved mud-mound preparation for coconut cultivation, preparing beds for kitchen garden which is part of agricultural activity and were clearly ineligible activities under NREGS. Similarly, a government cattle breeding farm had used NREGS funds for growing fodder on land within its campus. One instance of diversion of the scheme to benefit an ineligible person came to the notice in Chandrapini village, Edathiruthy GP, where a 3.5 hectare land owned by a well-off person lying fallow for 20 years was being reclaimed with NREGS funds. The scheme was promoted by the GP. In order to justify this diversion, one-year land lease agreement between the owner and the local women's SHG group of 20 members had

been entered whereby the latter could take up agricultural activities for generating income. Under Kudumbshree programme of the State Government, the SHG would be entitled to subsidies of seed, fertilizer and loan for taking up agricultural work. This was a smart ploy to not only reclaim long-unused, fallow land of a rich land owner, but also make it agriculture-worthy and profitable asset through government subsidy. The terms of lease and rent charges were not known. The owner could reclaim his land after expiry of the lease terms. In another place too, an instance of Kudumbshree groups leasing in private land and using NREGS labour for cultivation was observed.

It was learnt that a number of cases of land development works on land owned by APL households were taken up since they were small and marginal farmers. Instances of MGNREGS funds being used for land levelling and water conservation in a private college and on private farms were also noticed. The undertaking of NREGS works on private land was justified by *panchayat* functionaries and officials in Thrissur District on the ground of non-availability of public/government land. This was clearly a violation of the NREGS programme guidelines.

In Patwali village (Mathaser GP) of Narmada, out of 60 *khaatedaar*s, 20 land holders' land was uncultivable. Of them, 15 land levelling cases were taken up involving expenditure of ₹18 lakh. The one case the visiting team had a chance to inspect hardly qualified for it. It was an already cultivable field, next to the village entry road. The *medh* had been cut and the field slightly extended, hardly a land development exercise. In Bagdari GP of Sarguja District, land levelling of a two-acre land (out of total 12 acres) owned jointly by five brothers had been taken up. Conversations revealed that the brothers had several plots, broken up into small, scattered and unidentifiable pieces. The brothers were separate households. One of them desired that his share of plots could be made into one easily identifiable plot. Before taking up the scheme, it was necessary that proper division of land among brothers was effected by the revenue department. In the absence of proper demarcation of share and mutation of land, the work would generate avoidable dispute. In a joint holding, without consent of all stakeholders, taking up land development for one cultivator could lead to friction and even litigation.

Several of the land development cases taken up on tribal land suffered from low level of investment and were of little benefit. In Kakna village/GP (Sarguja) for example, tribal beneficiaries told the visiting team that putting a ceiling of ₹50,000 for land development schemes had led to incomplete land development of their plots. On one beneficiary's plot of two acres, work worth ₹10,000 only was taken up. He desired that sufficient work be sanctioned so that the entire area could be made cultivable. This type of land development was farcical and lacked technical input in preparation of schemes, its cost estimates and supervision during implementation.

In several cases, where land levelling cases had to be selected among a large number of aspirants, the very poor did not get a priority. Those whose lands were totally fallow, uncultivable and not being utilized needed to be accorded topmost priority. Rather, the better-off among them got it, probably because of better clout with the officials. Land development projects also suffered from standardized estimates unrelated to the site. There was no pre-measurement or site visits for taking up land development work.

In Sarguja District, land development was taken up on a large scale but seemed inappropriately executed. This scheme, it was informed, had the maximum demand. In Purkela GP and Batwahi village, several cases of land levelling were taken up on forest *patta* land. What was seen here was mere top soil removal, *medh* formation and some slope cutting. The quality of works was very poor. In Batwahi, a huge boulder had been left behind in the small plot belonging to a tribal. Below his land, where the slope ended, there was a beautiful natural water conservation spot on common land which had not been developed despite demand of villagers. Individuals through their own hard labour had bunded the stream by forming a mud wall.

Overall, officials implementing the scheme had no idea of land development. There were no guidelines, no training, no technical inputs and supervision going into it. Land development schemes are for agricultural activity but were sanctioned by civil engineers which was not their job. The very fact that mere ₹5,000–7,000 per scheme was sanctioned for each beneficiary was virtually a waste of funds. Also, since land was being allotted to tribals on a large scale, even in individual cases of land levelling, their harmonious integration with the watershed had to be kept in mind so that benefits could flow to all the plot holders in the watershed as a result of its restoration. Besides, since a number of beneficiaries were given *patta*s, their land development should have been taken up as a composite area for watershed planning. It would have also been cost effective. But the entire slope—comprising lands of several people—was not developed. Instead, one or two scattered/isolated plots were taken up which would ultimately not benefit the developed land as the passage of water and direction of its had not been taken into account.

In Vizianagaram District, in a tribal GP of Seetanagaram Block, land development of 50 farmers who had been given forest *patta*s in adjacent areas was identified for NREGS work. The plots each were of 1 to 1.5 acres and work on 24 of them was completed in 2011–12. The area was undulating and rainfall-dependant and most of the beneficiaries were poor, solely dependent on selling minor forest produce (leaves, firewood, etc.) for survival. In such a situation, it was important to promote their SSS in order that they could get assistance of different schemes for cultivation of land. Better still, joint farming could be experimented if the mates of different SSSs came together and mobilized the farmers for it. This would enable farmers to undertake joint planning on how best to utilize their land, pool their labour and collectively strive to get various services. At present, farmers buy seed and fertilizer, arrange cattle plough and get a well sanctioned individually. As a group, they could exert pressure to get entitlements from agriculture, animal husbandry and other departments delivered to the members. While taking up land development scheme it was also important to think about the capacity of the beneficiary to utilize the asset in order that the investment made in developing the land is not wasted. In one case, the area of land development taken up was large which the beneficiary, along with his family labour, would not be able to cultivate.

In several places, it was observed that a large area of government land (say in Keonjhar and Salem Districts) was lying unutilized in villages, unnoticed by officials and *panchayat* functionaries. Productive use could be made of this land under NREGS (such as social forestry) for the benefit of the village community. While developing individual land was most important to ensure livelihood security for the poor, an equally important facet of developing common/government land for larger benefit of community under NREGS was not considered. Nowhere did the visiting team find articulation of the need for development of community assets from available resources, from officials leaving aside water bodies.

Utilization of land after its development is important for the poor farmers as it is a source of livelihood. It was observed at several places, particularly where *patta*s were issued to tribals under the FRA, that government officials were pressurizing the beneficiaries to utilize it for plantation (horticulture, rubber, tea) rather than letting them decide. Most of them would rather grow food crops which would provide food security. Plantation crops do not yield immediate income and the grower is faced with problem of access to markets and remunerative pricing.

In earthen/field/rural connectivity road works, it was observed in at least three places (Dhamtari and Vizianagaram Districts, for instance) that earth (the good top soil) was being excavated from the adjacent fields of farmers (possibly tribals). Earth should be taken from the waste land, which was easily available near by, than from the farmer's field, as it would erode its fertility. It takes a long time for top soil to be formed which contains vital nutrients within it. This sensitivity in implementing officials was lacking.

2.9 CONVERGENCE ISSUES

Convergence of programmes is important in order to provide optimum benefits from the asset created to the targeted persons to enable them to improve their economic condition and rise above the poverty line. The most common model of convergence revolved around productive use of land through provisions of an irrigation source (well, farm pond and distribution of pump set) and making available seeds, fertilizers and technology.

In Narmada, through convergence, around 600 diesel pump sets were distributed to beneficiaries on whose land dug-wells had been constructed under NREGS. As some farmers had opted for horticulture and vegetable cultivation, a few of them were also provided sprinkler and drip irrigation from another department under its scheme. But the community wells are a misnomer. Usually three landholders are required to form a group. Actually, three cultivators within the same family join to claim this benefit (for example, in Vaadva village in Narmada). Since it was a community asset, it was important that other members whose plots lay adjacent to the well should be included in the group or allowed to use the water so that the asset was optimally utilized. The inputs and technology admissible under the existing schemes of the Ministry of Agriculture should also be provided.

A good example of this convergence was observed in Dhar District where ST *patta* holders under the FRA were assisted for land development and construction of well and schemes of sericulture, horticulture and fisheries departments were converged with it. This had helped in making productive use of land and bringing new land under cultivation. But examples of such effective convergence were very few.

Besides, convergence, wherever attempted, remained confined to land-based activities which left out landless rural poor from being targetted.

2.10 NREGS WORKS BY FOREST DEPARTMENT

In all States, forest department is an important line department to which substantial NREGS funds are transferred for taking up schemes which provide employment to forest dwellers and for creating assets useful to them. It was observed in tribal blocks in Narmada, Chhattisgarh District and Salem District that the forest department did not generate sufficient work through schemes under NREGS. On the other hand, it also did not allow revenue or *Panchayati Raj* departments to take up NREGS work in their areas. Additionally, it imposed severe restrictions on taking up works relating to construction of roads, water bodies or treatment of ridge in watershed development that could be taken up in the area under its domain. In fact, some of the schemes taken up by it were solely meant for wildlife and of no direct benefit to villagers (except wages).

In most of the habitations located in the forest or in its vicinity, land claims under the FRA were: (1) pending, (2) where a few *pattas* had been given, the area was drastically reduced against claims made and (3) claims not filed due to lack of information/awareness about the FRA or competence. Where *pattas* were issued and (such) land made cultivable with NREGS support, the forest department was imposing its choice on what beneficiaries could grow on it. Wage payment was also delayed in forest department schemes.

All information relating to budget, expenditure, man-days generated and works taken up was only provided at the district level to the DPC by DFOs and not shared with the block *panchayat*, GP or GS. The DPC has not ensured that the information is shared with the block/GPs.

In Khoda Amba (Ambavadi GP), in Normada, in a forest village comprising 120 households, 105 people had filed claims for issuance of *patta* under the FRA. Not one claim had been approved and the matter has been pending for three to four years. While claimants are *adivasis* and have been dwelling here since much before 2005, yet, against the FRA rules, the forest department was asking them for their proof of residence. The District Collector who is the Chairman of the district level committee under the FRA has not yet resolved this issue. Only 50 families had got about 11–13 days of work in 2011–12 (that too in December) and the wage realized was a little less than ₹100 (as against the NREGS rate of ₹124). In a nearby village, 110 of 120 households were landless and because of lack of livelihood opportunities, several of them went to Ankaleshwar and Surat in search of work. Also no entries were made in passbooks relating to NREGS work executed by the forest department. Payments were delayed for a month or more. In some places, forest department officials had kept job cards of people in their custody. There was lot of scope for work relating to watershed development under NREGS here.

In Kokti village (a settlement in sanctuary area) in the same district, where only the forest department executed NREGS work, only construction of rubber wall and *nala* bunding for the benefit of wildlife were taken up. Here, people complained about not getting work, job cards being kept by the forest department, work in their village being assigned to people from adjacent village (Samot), pending wage payment and the post master charging ₹10 for disbursement of wage to the beneficiaries. In a neighbouring village of Sissa, only 15 days of employment had been provided in the current year and 20 days during the last year (2010–11). Wage payment by the forest department was delayed by one month and 17 days this year, in comparison to four months during 2010–11. Since the forest department did not allow any other agency to operate, villagers were completely dependent on forest officials for work. The problems of such settlements needed to be sorted out by the DPC. In Narmada, MGNREGS funds were being used by the forest department without following any provision of the Act. There was also no supervision.

Some of the forest villages were so remote, poorly connected and distant from the GP office that officials either did not initiate work, or were not able to supervise it. One such was Talapada village in Baraigoda GP of Harichandanpur (Keonjhar), about 9 km from the block headquarters. No work was taken up here and officials complained that they faced problems in seeking permission from the forest department to undertake works. People had got only 12 days of work this year, in the nursery of the forest department. People also complained of low wage realization. They earned around ₹60–70 per day. Only eight to nine persons out of 120 households had land; nearly 173 had applied for *patta*s under the FRA last year and their claims were still pending. Several people had not been issued job cards.

In Singur GP (Dhamtari), the visiting team saw huge fencing (near Birjhuli/Birmuli road) of cemented poles on one side of the main road to protect forests from grazing by cattle (reared by the villagers) though there was no village in the immediate vicinity. It could not be verified whether NREGS funds were used for this fencing. In Sarguja District, roadside [either side of the highway/*Pradhan Mantri Gram Sadak Yojana* (PMGSY) roads] plantations using brick tree-guards were constructed on massive scale using NREGA funds. Bamboo or shrub fencing could have been cost effective. While brick tree-guards were proposed by the forest department, it had the approval of the State Government which issued a centralized directive for taking up this work, and funds for the same were allocated to the *panchayat*. No *panchayat* opposed the plantation scheme. The funds used in this scheme could have been better utilized for productive assets in the villages.

Instances of the forest department forcing change of land use was observed. In Dhalai, conversion of *jhum* lands into fruit orchards or bamboo plantations by the forest department without informed consent came to notice. Tribal beneficiaries of land *patta*s under the FRA were in a way being forced (through subsidy/induced demand) by the forest department to take up tree plantation of the latter's choice (as pineapple and banana) on their land rather than using it for food crops. Earlier, the tribals were doing *jhum*ing on their land, which is no longer permitted. This has not only affected their food security and freedom to use their land, but also led them to dependence on the market. It will lead to loss of gene pool of food-based crop grown on *jhum* lands in these areas, implying permanent loss in terms of biodiversity.

In the same district, instances of the bamboo seedling scheme and the FRA beneficiaries being made to raise horticulture plantation in which labour component was 3% and material component 97% were observed.

In Sarguja District, in one village, the visiting team came across the instance of FRA *patta* beneficiaries not knowing where their land was. While they had got the *patta*, land had not been demarcated due to negligence of the revenue department. These beneficiaries could not get the benefit of land development under NREGS. The programme officer failed to coordinate with the concerned department (forest/revenue) for demarcation of land.

In Malkangiri District, which is largely a forest region, the forest department was not involved in MGNREGS work.

In Narmada District, in several areas there was a tussle between the forest department and villagers on grazing issues. In one such area, the forest department had constructed ecotourism huts and employed 25–30 people on daily wage/contractual rates. In one such hut which the team visited, NREGS wage labour was used for land levelling, beautification and landscaping. This type of scheme did not have relevance for addressing people's problems which mostly relate to access to grazing issues and employment.

There is need for the Government of India to issue guidelines on what type of schemes in forest (areas) can be taken up with NREGS funds.

Across the districts, awareness about filing claims for forest land (*patta*) under the FRA was very low. It was learnt in some villages in Keonjhar, Dhamtari and Sarguja Districts that a lot of tribals had not even filed their claims because they were not aware of the law and procedure to put up a claim before the FRA Committee. The district administration should look into it. In several places where claims had been filed, these had been pending for years. In several cases where *patta*s were sanctioned, there was a drastic reduction in the allocation of land vis-à-vis the claim submitted. Additionally, a good number of claims were rejected and petitioners had not re-submitted them for review due to lack of knowledge. Officials should have intervened to seek cooperation of the forest department in solving these problems.

2.11 SCHEDULE OF RATES (SoR) AND WAGE REALIZATION ISSUES

There were no uniform SoRs for works undertaken under NREGS. As NREGS works are executed by different line departments (agriculture, forest, PWD, water resources, etc.) and *panchayat*, each of them used its own departmental SoR which were in variance with one another in terms of both work output and wages. Some were high, some were low. Also, these SoRs were formulated in the context of contract-labour work than for unskilled wage labour as in the case of NREGS.

This was causing severe disadvantages to the poor and leading to several distortions such as low realization of wages particularly after doing hard physical labour in tough soil conditions. It has also led to: (1) differential wage realization under different schemes, (2) inflated estimation of work in terms of man-days and wage cost, (3) low output of work and (4) labour opting out of NREGS work taken up by *panchayat*s.

In Nizamabad District, wage realization for different categories of work varied. It was more in cases of soft soil work (up to ₹120) and much less in case of hard soil work. Villagers complained that in the same village, some groups end up getting more, some less. In *mandal*s and GPs in the backward region of Telengana, people openly complained of not getting remunerative wages. In Pedagulla, where not much work was taken up last year, on being asked why people were not coming for NREGS work, they replied: '*Tees, chaalis rupay gir rahe hain, is liye*' (Wages under NREGS work out to ₹30 to ₹40, so we do not come). Some others said, 'Hard soil area *hai, is liye* rate *baraabar nahin hai*' (It is a hard soil area. Therefore, realization of wages is not equal to other areas). This was not so last-to-last year perhaps when they were able to get ₹110 from the work output. They also pointed out that, 'Tractor *bhar ke thekedaar le jaata hai logon ko*' (Contractor takes away tractor-load of people from here) to work elsewhere. They were taken on daily wages to locations around 10–15 km away and dropped back in the evening.

In Chillangi, Narsaagaud, where there were 73 SSS groups in 65 habitations, several people opted for transplantation of paddy work and 100–200 people from SCs going to Hyderabad in search of work. Here too, work was hard and wage realization under NREGS was low, forcing them to opt for farm labour, where wage was only ₹65. In Sadrabadi GP in Maleghat (Amravati), having majority of SC population (358 households) in a field road work, average wages realized were between ₹70 and ₹80 last year as against the stipulated rate of ₹105 for 2010–11.

In Tibla colony of Irulur tribals (Kemurur habitation) in Kadayampatti Block of Salem District, people complained of getting low wages even after completing pre-marked/assigned work. In case of hard soil it was difficult to complete the task, more so because a majority of labourers were women. While they were able to adhere to SoR norms in case of pond work, they could not do so in case of road work. In 2010–11, the average wage realization was ₹78–80 while for this year it was around ₹89.

In Patoli village and Samadpada GP (Narmada), officials told the visiting team that the issue of different SoRs of PWD and forest department had been raised in their block too. SoR norms of the forest department and their works (say nursery work, bund preparation, etc.) were milder and labourer-friendly and wages paid were much higher (at ₹124). In comparison, SoR of PWD was harsher.

2.12 WORKS RELATING TO WATER BODIES AND WATERSHED

In water storage/harvesting schemes such as ponds, tanks and bunds, compacting and pitching of loose earth was missing. Bunds needed to be strengthened, turfed and compacted. In many places, there were problems of design, choice of sites and lack of depth, all of which pointed to lack of sufficient technical input. It also highlighted lack of consultation with local people whose inputs of traditional knowledge and native wisdom could have corrected these faults.

In Rajivnagar *tanda* (habitation) of Ootapally village (Nizamabad District), there was a very good water body, renovation of which could have been shaped better. Because the foreshore had not been developed properly, it was getting silted. A lot of dirt and filth had accumulated in it because of lack of maintenance. In Pandapara village of Gathagaon Block (Keonjhar District), the visiting team saw a big community pond constructed last year. Villagers said it had the capacity to hold water throughout the year. However, its construction was faulty and a breach had occurred. It had four-side bunding but no escape. An outlet for discharge of surplus water had not been provided and its weakest point had not been identified.

In Chandi and Islampur Blocks of Nalanda District, traditional water bodies called *Ahars* and *Pynes* had been encroached upon by land owners leading to high run-off, flood and drought. The mode of irrigation system over time shifted from use of surface water to exploiting underground water. MGNREGS provided an opportunity to re-excavate these water bodies. About 482 *Pynes* were re-excavated in the year 2010–11 resulting in a significant increase in the irrigation potential of the entire district. Reviving the traditional irrigation system has increased the recharge capacity of ground water and availability of water during *rabi* cropping, and there is a two-fold increase in the area under irrigation. The storage capacity has also been augmented from 1.57 lakh m³ to 37.14 lakh m³ in the year 2009–10, as per government officials.

Nanded District took up water harvesting and water conservation works as the major developmental programme for reviving the ground water table, recharging the existing wells and arresting the run-off water through *Vanarai bori bundha* system. The soil and moisture conservation works executed in the last two to three years have improved the ground water table in the district, as the district received normal rainfall only during 2010–11. In Nanded, around 14,414 *Vanarai bandhara*s were constructed during the same year. The team was informed that due to the dug well recharging and other water harvesting structures, additional 30,000 hectares of *rabi* crop area had been brought under cultivation. The small and marginal farmers' purchasing power had considerably improved due to change in cropping system (from rain-fed crops to irrigated crops and also subsistence farming to commercial farming) mainly due to assured life-saving irrigation facilities wherever it could be available due to recharge of water bodies as a result of these interventions, according to officials.

In Kudipatti-Malaikonda (Salem District), a tribal village, the visiting team saw the rare sight of 200 workers engaged in desilting of a 100-acre pond and digging of lead channel over a large area, much of which had recently been freed of encroachment. Ten years ago, it used to be full of water. Though the scheme was approved by the Assistant Engineer, the pond's shape looked distorted and its gradient did not appear uniform. For some reason, tree plantation on one of its sides, at the base of a nearby hill, was taken up. This would create barrier for smooth flow of rainwater down the hill slope to the pond. The plantation and channel being created were hence in conflict with each other. Also, this project did not seem to optimally utilize land or the rainfall water available for harvesting. Since it was the *panchayat* land, a portion of it could be used for cultivation. Some scheme had been taken up on it years ago but was abandoned. There was a need to review this scheme by a watershed/agricultural expert.

In Karpannampatti (Umarganli GP of Salem District), a huge scheme of desilting a lake was in operation. Here also, it seemed to be an odd shape for a pond. While there was a field measurement book sketch of the lake, this was an ideal case for using satellite imagery for ascertaining the natural network of various channels feeding the lake, and figuring out those which had got blocked over the years. It had the capacity to hold huge amount of water. This required linkages between the concerned departments and the district-level planning agency.

Watershed principle was largely not being adhered to in taking up of water development schemes, thereby leading to suboptimal benefits of water bodies and land development activities. In Amlipaar village, Bhotapa GP (Dhamtari District), there was a need to develop plantations on the ridge forming the high ground of the local tiny watersheds. Water had to be arrested in higher reaches. Also, an area plan had to be made.

As a general rule, wherever wells or ponds were being dug, especially in large numbers in a single village (such as in Keonjhar District), recharging structures were missing. It was required to make it an integral part of water harvesting structures to prevent ground water depletion and drying up of the wells and ponds. The need for water recharging structures simultaneously with well construction was needed.

Panuda village (a winner of Nirmal puraskar for sanitation) in Narmada District was a spot for perfect watershed at the tri-junction of a tributary of Curzon River. It had a perennial source of water which was unutilized. The river bed was also getting silted, and land around it was fallow due to lack of irrigation and restrictions imposed by the forest department. A little lifting of water by using pump sets was required, which could be used for irrigation. It had the potential for a check dam too. Around 60–70 families required land levelling here. Villagers were not aware that they could seek assistance for digging of wells and pump sets. Overall, unknown to officials and people, here was an ideal village for undertaking affirmative action and convergence programmes which was not considered in local planning.

In Gohan *nala* village of Munaikera *panchayat* (Nagori Block, Dhamtari), three separate ponds, adjacent to each other, below the slope of a forest and at some distance from the village were constructed through *shramdaan*. It was on the land of Patels, the influential class. However, these too were technically flawed as rainwater spilled over in the monsoons. Adequate compacting of the foreshore (*medh*) had not been done, leading to cracks in walls and spillage of water. No channels (*naali*) had been constructed to take water to the fields. Due to scarcity, the water was used only for drinking purposes, both cattle and people. It seemed strange that despite construction of so many ponds, no irrigation water was available to villagers. In Bataurli village (Barinakela GP) of Sarguja, the site selection for a pond being constructed on a revenue land seemed inappropriate. In between fields and adjacent to ravine channels, it did not seem to be a natural storage point of water. In fact, it was obstructing a natural channel taking water to people's fields. While the Rural Engineering Services (RES) department had sanctioned it and the visiting teams was told the Sub-Divisional Officer (SDO) had seen the site, it is surprising that this flaw could not be observed by them. It raised the question about technical inputs into siting of the scheme.

In Munaikera (village/GP) of Sarguja, which was inside the forest area, the visiting team came across a unique initiative of tribals to construct a check dam, connecting tiny watersheds, which held rainwater on the slopes in their village. The village faced scarcity of water despite receiving good rainfall. Elders in the village had felt that there was sufficient run-off water during the rainy season which needed to be given a direction for harvesting it in a single place. They had tried earlier through *shramdaan* but failed as the previous spot sighted did not turn out to be accurate. They had come up with an alternative site and prepared a detailed plan for the new water body/check dam which would benefit three villages. They were trying to get the plan approved by officials. '*Ye agar paas ho jaae to hamaare gaon ka bhavishya sudhar jayega*' (If it is sanctioned, then the future of our village will be improved), said one expressing hope. If agencies vet this scheme of land and water resources development after investigation, it could prove to be very useful. Villagers also lamented that water harvesting structures were not being planned on the basis of people's traditional knowledge.

In Bagdari village (Surguja District), a good water tank was seen on which deepening work had stopped with the onset of rains due to the government circular preventing work from June onwards till September–October due to rains leading to wastage of incomplete work. If the work had been taken up sufficiently before the onset of monsoon, this wastage could have been avoided. Timing of taking up such works was important, as break in (earth) work due to rains led to wastage of work (done) and inefficiency of expenditure. Ideally, the GP should set a predetermined time period for completing such works and preferably take it up from October onwards.

In Kakna village in the same district, pond deepening work was required to store the water that was readily available and now flowing away. However, due to a ceiling on expenditure of ₹1 lakh to 1.5 lakh for such works by the district administration, the *panchayat* could not take it up. The pond overflows in the rains, villagers told the visiting team. They had never explored the idea of forming earthen channels (*kacchi naali*) to route its water to their fields.

In several districts, the team chanced upon good sites for storage of water. There were also several existing water bodies in derelict condition, silted or taken over by weeds. Such conditions also made them susceptible to encroachment. Since these were in irrigation-scarce areas, they held a lot of potential for being developed as a community resource under NREGS. Also, a watershed expert at the district level was needed to undertake planning of all water-related works in each of the blocks of the district within the framework of tiny watershed in which they were located. Land development and tree plantation could also be combined by applying the ridge-to-valley principle. Civil engineers and agriculture experts are not adequately oriented and trained towards watershed development.

2.13 WOMEN AND GENDER ISSUES

Even in the places where there was a large turnout of women workers (say in the southern States) and where there were SSS groups to mobilise them (say in Andhra Pradesh), the team hardly came across women mates anywhere. This exclusion of women workers from leadership role needed to be addressed. Worksite facilities such as crèche and shade for them were almost entirely absent.

In Narmada, the visiting team was told that in the construction of wells, the women's participation was 40–50%. This is so even in deep-digging—the toughest part—of work. In Paddayar GP, Eddtirinji colony (Thrissur District), where work availability was scarce (NREGS is the only option available), women labourers were observed cleaning a weed (water hyacinth)-infested water channel while immersed chest-deep in water. No protective gear had been given to them. They were also demanding that this work be stopped as it created skin rashes and was tough. However, what appeared incongruous was that it was not clear why the water channel was being cleared as lands on either side of it had since long been lying fallow. Officials intimated that it was an old channel, part of a canal system which had fallen into disuse over the years and abandoned. Due to water logging, it had become a breeding ground for mosquitoes. The cleaning work would allow free movement of water, help control floods and improve health conditions in the area, the officials told the visiting team.

In certain *panchayat*s of Salem and several in Thrissur, the number of days women had worked as reflected in the MIS and what the women actually reported during conversation, pointed towards a large gap. Possibly incorrect data was being fed into the MIS, though this needs further investigation. In one instance while the MIS showed 65–85 days of work per woman worker, it was somewhere around 40 when we enquired from women job card holders.

Even though several *panchayat*s were headed by women, the team did not find any contribution from them towards greater sensitivity for gender-related issues in NREGS implementation. This calls for training and capacity building of women *panchayat* representatives, and particularly *sarpanch*s.

2.14 SUSPECT NREGS WORKS

In Narmada, a large number of compost pits within boundaries of individual households had been sanctioned at an estimated cost of ₹25,000–30,000. No muster rolls were being maintained for this work. These indeed were very small pits, and did not qualify for an investment worth the aforesaid amount. Also, any NREGS work should involve a minimum of 10 wage seekers which was not happening in this case.

In Thavali Shahid GP of Amravati District, nearly 200 fruit trees had been planted on the *shamshan* (cremation ground) land belonging to the *panchayat*. Nearly 40 families were involved in watering, trimming bushes and tending of these trees. Since three years, in batches of five persons in one lot, each was being paid ₹127 per day for 100 days of continuous work, the money being booked under NREGS. This was a privileged work since it did not involve hard labour. Also, it was more like a continuous employment for them and most inequitable distribution of work. Only some workers close to the staff got this benefit. Ideally, this type of soft work should have been rotated among the most vulnerable workers (such as older and disabled persons or those suffering from some ailment).

In Eriad (GP), a coastal area village in Thrissur affected by tsunami a few years ago, under NREGS work, a wall of sand-filled plastic sacks was being created to reduce the force of waves and prevent sea water ingress into the village. The utility of such work was suspect as the sand wall would be no match to the force and height of sea water waves and would get washed off during high tide. A better idea would have been to treat this space by a boulder protection wall (which already exists in patches) under a flood protection scheme.

Casuarina plantation had also been taken up on land in coastal areas, much of which was heavily encroached. For their maintenance, NREGS funds were being used. About ₹7 lakh was spent in watering the trees for the last three years and may continue for another year. It was not clear what the community gain was of this project. No information was available about the survival rate of these trees. While tree plantation can be taken up under NREGS on public land, the choice of species and their utility to the local population should be kept in view and discussed in the GS. This put question mark on selection of schemes, participation and deliberation in the GS and the decision-making process.

The nature of schemes taken under NREGS in Thrissur District did not add up to something substantial. Small-duration works (schemes) were taken up which hardly lasted a week or so. Some did not qualify for NREGS works. Say for instance, the scheme labelled as canal cleaning was cleaning of drains running in front of the *pucca* houses. There was no desilting involved in the residential colony. It was simply scraping of grass. No trace of agricultural land could be seen nearby. Similarly, preparing five cents of land for kitchen garden and mound preparation for coconut plantations were doubtful work under NREGS. The visiting team did not come across durable assets being created under NREGS in the district.

2.15 OTHER ISSUES

In one of the *taluka*s of Amravati District, it was observed that wage payment under NREGS was way above the stipulated rate. As high as ₹266 per individual (in certain cases) was being paid. It was justified by officials arguing that the worker had put in requisite work. This is not in consonance with NREGS guidelines.

In the Rajiv Gandhi Bhavan(s) constructed across districts, information about NREGS scheme, names of officials, work hours, phone numbers, applications, dates of payment and latest information was not displayed. There were no boxes for receiving work demand applications. It was important that whatever information is needed to be given to people should be put on display on the walls. People should not be dependent on officials for accessing information.

The Maharashtra Government circular charging royalty fee for mud works done on individual beneficiaries' land (as witnessed in Rajur and Amla GPs in Amravati District) needed to be brought to the issue of the Ministry of Rural Development (MoRD). Also, the new MoRD circular detailing eligibility criterion for individual work had to be specifically brought to the notice of the State Government.

Consolidated district reports

The reports that follow emerge from the methodology of field investigation laid down by the Award Committee. As a first step, the Committee decided to have oral presentations from District Programme Coordinators (DPCs) of the districts recommended by the respective State Governments for the award. They were asked to indicate their performance in respect of major objectives of the programme such as participation of beneficiaries through the GS, number of days of employment provided, timely payment of wages, social equity, reduction in distress migration, rejuvenation of local natural resources base for support of livelihood systems, creation of community assets, improvement in productive resources of SCs/STs, women's participation, governance issues such as planning, timely flow of resources, accountability of officials, quality of works, maintenance and updating of records, etc.

The Committee evaluated their performance based on these presentations and shortlisted the districts for field checks to verify the claims made therein. The Committee constituted teams for each district consisting of two to four persons (members and experts). During these visits, effort was made to visit all blocks of the district covering at least two *panchayats* in each of them as far as possible. Usually, some officials from the district and block accompanied the team during these visits. Each member of the team visiting a block looked into the performance of the *panchayat* on the basis of data provided in the MIS and then selected the villages for talking to the workers and *panchayat* functionaries, verifying the job cards, inspecting the records and assessing the quality of works. He also discussed labour budget, allocations received, money spent, pendency of schemes, etc. with the *panchayat*/block officials. During the discussion with the workers it was ascertained whether they were able to get

work on demand and the time taken in payment of wages, etc. On return to the district head quarters, impressions of the visit were shared with district officials and clarifications, if any, were sought. The information collected by the team members for different blocks was reported individually to the chairperson. The district reports were discussed in the Committee for the purpose of making selection for the Award. These reports were thereafter compiled, integrated in respect of each district and edited. Thereafter a consolidated report was prepared analyzing evidence emerging from them under certain broad themes. It was concluded with a list of recommendations for improving the execution of the programme addressing the shortcomings highlighted in the consolidated report. The following sections consist of reports of the team in respect of 19 districts visited during the year.

3.1 REPORT OF NATIONAL COMMITTEE FOR MGNREGS ADMINISTRATIVE AWARDS 2010–11: ALAPPUZHA DISTRICT (KERALA)[1]

Observations

Given the environment in Kerala where wage rates are high at around ₹300 per day for women and up to ₹500 per day for men, the level of participation of rural households in MGNREGS works is rather low. The GPs are doing their best to identify suitable worksites, but the size of land holdings being again very small and such land holdings being available only with better-off sections of the rural community, there is a serious problem of grounding MGNREGS

[1] This report has observations of Hemnath Rao, Nilay Ranjan, B. Panda (who went together) and Reetika Khera who visited the district.

works strictly according to the guidelines laid down in the Act. However, in the Alappuzha District from the field visit to two GPs each in two blocks, it was observed that 10–15 rural households formed a group and engaged themselves in regular agricultural operations on private farms. We also observed that most of the workers were getting wage on time. Maximum delay was observed in Maraikulam GP that is 30 days.

The whole team visited first the GP Maraikulam South in Maraikulam Taluk and then visited a worksite to see the programme implementation especially the convergence aspect. At this worksite, the NREGS work of planting of fodder grass was taken up in private land of an SC household. The quality of asset created through convergence was not very convincing. The measurement aspect was also not very sound and the technical assistant (TA) and the engineer were unable to convince me on this. Since the authorities had claimed wage payment in seven days, that aspect was enquired. It was found that the cumulative payments were made through post office and it was never made in seven days. However, the mobilization and equity aspects were visibly strong.

On 28 December 2011, Venmony *panchayat* and two worksites were visited. In the *panchayat* office, the NREGS record keeping and infrastructure are good. However, in both the worksites, payments are never made in seven days. It is made within 14 days. In the worksite of Aimthuruthu-Thenneerkolla Thodu, entries in many of the job cards were not made. For example, M.S. Soman having job card no. KL-11-005-008-806-67 has worked for last seven days but no entry was made in the job card. Job cards of many of the NREGA workers were not updated. Worksite facilities such as first aid, shade and crèche were not provided in both the worksites. In both the worksites, workers were hurriedly called to work just to showcase them to the visitors. The programme officer's involvement was casual.

Good practices

The advance payment after the closing of the muster without measurement is one of the good practices which help in reducing the hardship caused to the workers by delay in payment. The project diary being used by the mates is another good practice that shows the details of the project sanctioned and the milestones in the implementation of the project including the list of equipment used by the labourers and rental charges on equipment paid to the wage seekers. The diary also provides for workers' comments and observations by visiting officers.

At the end of the evaluation, it was obvious that good attention is being paid by the district team to the implementation of the programme particularly in regard to the identification of beneficiaries from SC and ST categories. The GPs are very well staffed and the process of planning and maintenance of records is admirable, which is more a reflection on the good status of PRIs than the MGNREGS project team.

Another good practice observed in the *panchayat* office is that it works like a mini Secretariat. All the important services are delivered at the *panchayat* office and the front room of the *panchayat* office works as information desk for the citizen. They also maintain proper record of all the welfare schemes.

The fact, however, remains that there is simply no farming activity happening in rural Kerala and using the MGNREGA wage seekers to develop private lands is a matter of serious concern as the land holdings belong to the APL families. It was also found that the job cards are not regularly updated though records are well maintained in the GP. Thus, there is no significant innovation or best practice to be observed that directly benefits the wage seekers or the disadvantaged sections of the society.

Good systems of implementing the programme are no substitute to sustainable outcomes that can promote livelihood security. While the demand is evident among women wage seekers, the programme remains supply driven. Hence, while we appreciate the programme implementation procedure at an aggregate level, there is no distinctive feature that the district administration could claim as benefitting the wage seekers on a sustained basis.

Challenges

Most of the works undertaken under MGNREGS are not sustainable and the district is using individual land of the non-resident Indians and other ineligible persons for MGNREGS works, which is a violation of the MGNREG Act. We observe that MGNREGS money is being used by local land owner for getting advantage in terms of field preparation for cultivation.

While the demand is evident among women wage seekers, the programme remains supply driven. We appreciate the programme implementation procedure at an aggregate level. The important thing which we observe is that the district administration is able to reduce the delay in wage payment.

Positive highlights

Two blocks namely Alappuzha and Mavelikara were visited. In Alappuzha, Mariakulam South GP and in Mavelikara, Thekkokkara GP, respectively, were covered.

Keeping in view the other areas of the country (Himachal Pradesh, Uttar Pradesh, Rajasthan, Bihar, Jharkhand, Chhattisgarh, Gujarat, Madhya Pradesh, Odisha, Andhra Pradesh and Tamil Nadu) that have been seen, the implementation of NREGA in the two districts in Kerala is certainly very impressive compared to that in most, and similar to what one sees in Tamil Nadu. However, it is worth bearing in mind that in both the Kerala districts, the visitor was escorted by the district officials and was probably shown the best they had, whereas in all other States the team visits have been independent and unannounced, so that they probably saw the worst as well in those States. The positive highlights are listed as follows:

1. **Massive participation of women in NREGA.** On the worksites, it is basically all women, but more encouragingly, women are to be seen in plenty at almost every conceivable post such as assistant engineers, overseers, data entry operators, *panchayat* presidents, mates, Block Development Officer (BDO). The *skill ladder* exists in some ways—a NREGA worker in Allapuzha whom we met was now elected as a block *panchayat* member.

2. **Real role for GPs in the planning and implementation process.** PRIs are super strong, with amazing infrastructure (GP offices resemble block offices of some of the northern States), and everything goes through them. They actually seem to prepare annual plans for each *panchayat* and follow the prioritization decided in the GS. The block *panchayat* has standing committees on different subjects. The blocks that were visited often had various block *panchayat* members who were there either because they were expecting a visitor from Delhi, or it seems that they are always around.

3. **Demand-driven process seems to be in place, at least partially.** At the visited worksites, the labourers were asked whether and where they apply for work. There is an application window at the *panchayat* office to receive applications. However, unemployment allowance is not paid. It is observed that awareness of this is also low.

4. **Quality of assets.** This is the truly remarkable feature of NREGS here. With Kudumbashree programme taking a massive interest in NREGS, every possible kind of convergence is taking place. But there are some caveats (see below). In Thrissur, the cattle breeding farm under the Veterinary University offers its land to the NREGS labourers where they work to grow fodder for the cattle. Canal maintenance and sluice gate maintenance were the other big works in Thrissur—desilting of canals means the canal can function for irrigation purposes, and also raises the water level in private wells. In Allapuzha, Kudumbashree groups grow vegetables, possibly paddy also, and the former is sold locally. It is also linked to the marketing agency (or whatever it is called) for selling in larger markets. Kudumbashree groups are learning how to farm for the first time. They lease in private land and use NREGA labourers for some part of their cultivation. Quite a lot of land development work is being undertaken on private and public lands. Another case of good work was the cleaning (desilting and de-weeding) of ponds in Allapuzha. Along with that, soil conservation works and water harvesting works are being undertaken with great thought. Under soil conservation, thought is being given to enhancing nitrogen content by adding certain leaves.

5. **Plantation of vettivar grass (magic grass).** This grass reduces pollution in ground water (including ridding it of pollutants from Vijay Mallaya's brewery in the neighbourhood). It also prevents soil erosion; apparently you can only remove it using JCB machines! Mud compacting is also done to enhance soil quality. Much of this is possible because they have enough agricultural scientists and engineers.

Negative highlights

There is some uncertainty in the visistor's mind as to whether some of the land development work basically boils down to subsidizing the cost of labour for private farmers, or whether this can still be justified as additional employment generated.

Participation of men is low primarily because of the low NREGA wage, so they prefer other work. The labour market seems to be segregated along gender lines.

Delays in payment of wages continue to be a problem though not at all like in the northern States. Here payments are made in 20–25 days according to district officials, who were quite candidly speaking about this. It seems that delays are at two stages—one, submission of paperwork by the mate to the GP gets delayed and two, cross measurement by the assistant engineer may be delayed.

Worksite facilities are very poor, often not provided. Updating of job cards is irregular and not updated. Payments are never made in seven days as claimed but generally do not exceed 14 days. Monitoring is very weak. Asset quality is poor.

3.2 REPORT OF NATIONAL COMMITTEE FOR MGNREGS ADMINISTRATIVE AWARDS 2010–11: AMRAVATI DISTRICT (MAHARASHTRA)[2]

Observations

The first village visited was Kohana in Chikaldhara GP of Maleghat subdivision. This subdivision is forested and predominantly tribal. Korku and Gond are the two main tribes inhabiting this region. The visitors went straight to the GP office where the *Gram Sevak* was available. About six to seven job cards with very old entries were lying with him. A blank payment sheet signed by the *panchayat* and other officials was also found in the file. Some families were visited. When the families were asked for their job cards they said they did not have these with them. In their post office passbooks, entries of payments were mentioned. The last payment entry was of July 2010. There were no entries for the year 2011. On enquiry it was found that people were willing to work but late payments of the wages worked as deterrent.

The second village visited was Salona. In the job card register with the *Rojgar Sevak*, there were entries of 395 job cards. Muster roll was corrected using white correction fluid extensively and so names had been changed. *Tehesildar* who is the project officer for the block had never attended any social audit. Old job cards issued during the Employment Guarantee Scheme (EGS) were available. Renewal of job cards had not taken place in the village. So, no new entry has been possible. Out of the total population of 100,000 persons, 18,000 are agricultural labourers and 6,000 have migrated outside their villages in search of employment. The NREGS work cycle period here is October to July.

Achalpur Block was visited. It consists of 70 GPs and 126 villages. Total population of the Block is 165,500, out of which 14,219 are landless labourers. About 20% population comprises SCs and 5% STs.

Rasgaon GP has 423 families, consisting of 116 SC families, 290 OBC families and 17 ST families. About 110 families are landless. There are 241 job card holders. For the year 2010–11, the village has undertaken only one work of field ponds on the field of an OBC farmer (who does not belong to SC, ST and BPL category). Beneficiary is the *sarpanch* of the GP. Maharashtra has added another category under individual beneficiary list—those farmers who received loan waivers fall in this category. Muster rolls were not available in the GP office. After sometime, the *Gram Sevak* brought it from his home. It was not updated. Labourers reported that they had worked for 10 days but muster roll record for four days was not available. People needed job but their job request was not responded to. They were not given any receipt for their demand.

People were not aware of the provision of the scheme. Payment was very much delayed. Sometimes it was delayed even beyond two months which dissuaded workers from seeking job under NREGS. There were 12 landless SC families who had been denied ration card. There was another plantation work undertaken on *panchayat* land. One person has been working for almost a year. He has been receiving his wages through other people's account and against others' names. No muster roll could be made available for this work. The *Gram Sevak* reported that he had taken these records for entry in the computer, so he was not in a position to show that record. He promised to bring after a few hours.

The next block visited was Ajangaon which has 49 *gram panchayat*s. About 11,832 job cards were issued in this block. It has got 86% literacy. The block office did not have data on landless families and families which migrate. Both the *Tehesildar* and BDO were new. They had recently taken charge. So far during the last year 2010–11, 44 works were completed in seven GPs. All these were 'pond filling' on private lands. Rajeev Gandhi Seva Bhawan was completed and no other works were taken up in the category of common community asset. A total of 16,497 persons got more than 100 days job in the year. About 44,240 person-days work was generated and the beneficiary break-up was SCs: 3,438, STs: 293 and others: 40,509 days.

Kasbegawahan *panchayat* was visited where tree plantation work was undertaken. **This was the only *panchayat* where all records relating to sanction and muster roll were maintained properly.** Job cards were available with the beneficiaries and these had up-to-date entry of wage payments. Workers were paid more than ₹127 per day also if they worked more and the lowest entry was ₹75. In one case, shortage of junior engineers (JEs) was also causing delay in measurement and certification leading to

---

[2] This report has mostly the comments of Dayaram with inputs of M.D. Asthana who visited the district. Please see the summary and theme-wise reports for comments of K.B. Saxena.

delay in payment. Beneficiaries complained that due to change in the payment procedure, wage payments were delayed. Many belonging to landless SC families reported that they were not given ration cards. On enquiry, the BDO and *sarpanch* both agreed that those who had complained deserved ration cards but due to faulty lists prepared they were denied and the Maharashtra Government had stopped issuing new ration cards for last more than one year.

Harishal *panchayat* in Dharni Block was visited. This *panchayat* is inhabited by tribals (90%). Main tribes are Kurku and Gond while Gawalis are non-tribals. More than 70% persons above 18 years old have migrated out of the village in search of work. They are working as labourers in brick kilns, *dal* mills and also in cotton fields. The *panchayat* falls under the reserve forest area and the *Gram Sevak* reported that there were hardly any possibilities of generating work. Most migrations were to cities such as Amravati and Nagpur and some even migrated to Mumbai as construction workers. Some of the women available in the village reported that they had to migrate due to non-availability of work in the village. Women generally collect fire wood and sell it in towns. Agricultural wage available in the area was ₹60 per day. The Forest Ranger reported that possibilities of creating work in reserved forest areas were extremely limited.

In Daryaganj Block which was visited, officials were of the view that the area had very high agricultural wage and due to that people did not want to work under MGNREGS. There were some *panchayats* where no NREGS work had been initiated so far for the stated reason. The visitor made request to visit one such *panchayat* and he was taken to Hirangaon *panchayat*. The village has 450 families consisting of SCs, STs and OBCs. Officials reported that they had offered work but no one was willing to take work under NREGS as agricultural wage in the area was very high and people found round-the-year work in agriculture. In the village meeting, when record of the job offered was asked for, there was nothing made available. People gathered in large numbers and on enquiry they reported that they were not given job cards so far, though they had applied for it. The *Gram Sevak* brought one beneficiary who said he had got a job card but he was unable to produce the same. People present there reported that the agricultural wage was low and not available throughout the year and so a substantial number of them migrated to towns and cities for work.

A bundle carrying job cards was found in the *almirah* which came out while locating the job order notice apparently they had issued. No one in the village was ever given job cards. These were all lying in the *panchayat* office. There was no meeting ever to explain the scheme in the village and people had no idea about it. Names on the job cards were read and people available there were given job cards by the BDO. The BDO was requested also to explain the crowd which had swelled to over 100 persons by this time about the NREGS. People complained that they were without work and they were being denied work saying there was no sanction from the high-ups. Next day again, two GPs—Mokhad under Nandgano and Shiagaon under Toesia Block—were visited.

Key points

Transition from the EGS to MGNREGA is yet to be understood by the *panchayat* and local functionaries. They are still working within the EGS framework, and the key processes in NREGS such as holding GSs, giving job cards to workers, maintaining muster rolls, holding social audits, etc. are not adhered to.

The Government of Maharashtra has also included farmers who were beneficiaries under the loan waiver scheme as beneficiary for work on individual work. This has led to most landed people getting free labour on their land under NREGA.

Migration continues to be on and the NREGS work does not seem to have impacted distress migration.

There seems a very deliberate attempt by functionaries to deprive people of work to keep the agricultural wages low and also ensure agricultural labourers available at low rates.

SC/ST and BPL families who have some land have not benefitted under provisions meant for them for work on personal land. Even that is being cornered by the landlords through the revision in the criteria.

In the social asset categories, roads and plantation works have been undertaken.

Record keeping is extremely poor. In most of the places visited, records were in a sorry state. Records including job cards were mostly in possession of village officials and incomplete.

No record was maintained of the employment demand and it being provided. The deman always matched with start of the work. Like everywhere else, there is not a single day of unemployment allowance ever paid. In fact, shockingly there is a general consensus that in times of keen demand of labourer for agriculture, NREGS work should not be started. This defeats the very purpose of the scheme. Land-owners get away with payment of wages which are lower than NREGS wages.

A very large number of works have been given to the line departments which still are living in the age of EGS. Their SoR is departmental. Measurement of works and hence wage entitlements/payments are severely delayed.

Inspection or supervision of NREGS works is poor because of lack of manpower. JE-level workers shockingly are allowed to work even in the private sector. Attention to NREGS works is accordingly poor, delaying measurements and payment of wages. They are untrained also. A very small number of job card holders are active workers. Because of poor system of supervision, there is doubt whether the workers reported working and to whom the payments are actually made are really working. If the tribal portion of the district is in a bad shape from every point of view, it is because of utter indifference of authorities including the Collector (who hardly seemed to be taking any interest in the programme and behaved as if he was an outsider, not a programme coordinator). If Amravati is one of the better performing districts, one shudders to think as to what is happening in rest of Maharashtra so far as MGNREGS goes.

3.3 REPORT OF NATIONAL COMMITTEE FOR MGNREGS ADMINISTRATIVE AWARDS 2010–11: COIMBATORE DISTRICT (TAMIL NADU)[3]

District profile

Coimbatore District is one of the more affluent and industrially advanced districts of Tamil Nadu. It is known as the Manchester of South India because it houses many textile industries. It has the highest gross domestic product (GDP) among the districts of Tamil Nadu, even ahead of the State capital Chennai. The rural people are mostly agriculturists, although with the advent of special economic zones (SEZs) in the area, service and IT industries are booming. It is the highest revenue-yielding district in the State. The district enjoys pleasant climate all throughout the year with heavy rainfall (700 mm) due to its association with the Western Ghats. It has a population density of 572 inhabitants per square kilometre. Its literacy rate is 69%. The district has 12 blocks. The major crops cultivated in the district are gingelly (34% share of Tamil Nadu), coconut, sugarcane, etc.

[3] This report has comments of V. Suresh Babu, Nilay Ranjan, B. Panda, Hemnath Rao and M.D. Asthana who visited the district.

Performance of MGNREGS in the district

The general performance of MGNREGS in the district can be considered satisfactory both in terms of number and variety of works viewed against the background that the district has a high number of urban blocks and many industries are dispersed around the Coimbatore town. Labourers migrate in large numbers out of interior rural areas and the district administration has made a concerted effort to respond to their demand for work during specific period when agricultural works are not active. Though the habitations are dispersed in each *panchayat*, transport allowance is being paid systematically to ensure reasonably good response from households. The BDOs and other project functionaries have regularly visited the villages and habitations to support the GP members in identifying potential works.

Total 1.60 lakh job cards have been issued in Coimbatore. It is noticed during the field visit that many of the households who are agricultural labourers or belonging to disadvantaged sections were denied of job cards. About 60% of job cards have been issued to other categories, 3.2% to STs and 36% to SCs. During 2010–11, 39.91 lakh person-days have been generated. Out of which SCs constitute 41%, STs 3% and others 56%. Women participation is very high with 85%. Based on the job cards issued, the person-days generated per household are 28 days for SCs, 22 days for STs and 24 days per household in total. As per the MIS information on 23 January 2012, 0.26% of households have completed 100 days of employment. Only one work has been completed under water harvesting and water conservation, while 2,244 works are listed under in-progress/suspended works and another 540 works are approved, not in progress. However, during the field visit it is found that many works have been completed under each category of permissible works. It appears that the MIS is not updated.

Improvement to the channel from Angamuthu-gounder *thotam* to check dam at Kurumbapalayam has been taken up at a cost of ₹1,142,051. A group of 20 members has to dig 12 m × 30 cm × 9 m size drains to earn their minimum wage. It appears that the agricultural wages have increased, in case of women from ₹50 to ₹120 per day and in case of men from ₹100 to ₹200. The agricultural wages depend upon the nature and time of operation. Availability of employment for the landless agricultural labourer is very limited as the entire hamlet has coconut orchards, a perennial crop, in which the labour requirement is very meagre. Hence, there is huge demand for MGNREGS works.

The wage seekers work from 9 a.m. to 3 a.m. (including an hour's lunch break) at worksite. It was interesting to note that the wage seekers had tied up with a tea shop, which served tea at 11.00 a.m. at worksite along with snacks.

It is found that every scheme estimate consists of jungle clearance component without considering its requirement at the worksite. Junior or assistant engineers are preparing the cost estimate without considering the worksite conditions. The cost estimate has made a provision for photographs of the site with an allocation of ₹1,240. However, asset registers do not contain any photographs (pre-, mid- and post-work photographs). In coconut orchards, usually, men are paid ₹300 and women are paid ₹150 per day for loading and unloading the lorry.

At several worksites, it is noticed that the last year approved works are being carried out without approval of the revised budget. The SoR has been revised for jungle clearance from ₹4.23/m² to ₹5.03/m² while the earth excavation has been increased from ₹61.20/m³ to ₹72.83/m³. At every worksite, it was found that there was a difference between estimated expenditure and actual expenditure of ₹3–4 lakh which could have been utilized towards generation of person-days of employment. In a few cases, the approved work (such as excavation of pond) has been replaced with alternative work as the pond is filled with water.

The major works executed under MGNREGS are as follows:

a. Channel improvement
b. Desilting of pond
c. Improvement of irrigation or drainage channel
d. Improvement of supply channel
e. Desilting of supply channel
f. Improvement of earthen rural connectivity
g. Formation of road
h. Formation of new pond

At Vellamadai worksite, Sarcarsamakulam Block, it is noticed that most of the wage seekers have crossed 100 days of employment. It is surprising to notice that the MIS has accepted more than 100 days against the individual wage seeker. Since more than 100 days is being accepted, who is bearing the additional wage burden—the Centre or the State Government? It is noticed that in none of the blocks, 30% additional wages for physically challenged person is not paid. The wage seekers are not covered under *Aam Admi Bima* and *Swasthya Bima Yojana*s.

Three block headquarters (Pollachi, Anamalai and Sultanpet) were visited. Records, data and reports were inspected. Interactions with the programme officers (POs) and other MGNREGS functionaries were held to evaluate the programme in terms of equity, inclusion, capacity building, monitoring and evaluation, grievance redressal, transparency and efficiency and conformation to MGNREGA norms and guidelines.

To know the actual field situation, offices and field sites in Divansapudar and Kaliyapuram GPs in Anamalai Block, Nattukkappalyam GP in Pollachi Block and Pachapalayam and Vadambacheri GPs in Sultanpet Block were visited. Worksites visited were: (i) Arjuna Garden deepening of pond, (ii) improvement to the earthen road from Mungiladi to Chellapilai Karada, (iii) improvement to the supply channel from Kasipattinam Nathakadu Thottam to N.K.K.T.S. Thottam and (iv) Thalinjikauakutti supply channel. The positive aspects observed are as follows:

(i) Records are updated and well kept in the offices of the PO as well as *panchayat*.
(ii) Social equity in works has been taken care of.
(iii) Payment made within eight days on the designated pay day, that is, Tuesday of the week.
(iv) Women and ST workers predominate MGNREGA work.
(v) Worksite supervisors take interest in the programme.
(vi) The Programme Director (PD) and the DPC are quite involved in MGNREGA.
(vii) Monitoring is satisfactory.

Affirmative action to enhance the participation of marginalized community

As per the State operational guidelines, individual works cannot be executed in SC/ST/BPL/IAY/Land reforms and small and marginal lands. The beneficiaries of land development activity are mostly OBCs holding less than 5 acre land. According to the MIS data 2010–11, only one work has been reported to be completed under water harvesting and water conservation category. However, several works have been executed under MGNREGS during 2010–11. The quality of works executed under MGNREGS is very good. Most of the works are executed on the community land only, especially earthen works.

Grievance redressal mechanism

It was informed that the social audit had been carried out twice in a year. No complaints have been reported either in the complaint register or in the social audit. The wages are paid in three to four days (maximum in a period of four to six days). Payments are made in cash. In case the wage seeker is not available at the GP office during wage disbursement, the wages are deposited in the wage seeker's account after two days.

Good practices

Since certain habitations faced the danger of wild animals straying into the village habitations causing damage to life and property, trenches conforming to the specifications prescribed by the forest department are excavated under MGNREGS to provide employment and at the same time prevent entry of wild animals. Revival of water tanks and deepening of supply channels have indeed improved the water table. Members of the Irulla tribe who were traditionally migrating to the nearby towns for livelihood are returning back to GPs due to the availability of work under MGNREGA. While inter-habitation equity is a matter of concern, the district administration has tried and encouraged people from more than one habitation to participate in MGNREGS works being implemented in a given habitation.

We could not find any distinct innovation or good practices implemented under MGNREGS. The MGNREGS is being executed in a team spirit.

Other observations

An effort was made to improve the quality of works with deeper involvement of the local community, particularly members of SCs and STs which helped achieve better enrolment of SC families in MGNREGA works. In Panni Madai GP of Periyanaichenpalayam Block, 120 families have completed 100 days of work of whom more than 50% were women belonging to SCs. A wage seeker by name Ms Sivagami working as a bonded labourer with a big farmer by name Mr Appu Gounder in the village could come out of the bonded status, thanks to the extra income which MGNREGS provided to her husband. The family belonged to the Irula tribe. Yet another interesting case was of Ms Margadam in the Mathampatty GP of Thondamuthur Block who enrolled her daughter for a Diploma Course in IT. She was also looking forward to her son completing his 10th class in the current academic year, which she attributed to the economic support that MGNREGS provided to her. This may be anecdotal evidence of the quality of programme implementation. However, considering the fact that these wage seekers were prone to migration to the nearby Coimbatore city but have now decided to stay back in the village and support their children's education is evidence, all

the same, of the positive outcomes emerging from the programme.

DPC and team performance

In spite of the restrictive nature of the guidelines of the State Government in the choice of MGNREGA works and the number of wage seekers who can be provided employment at any given point of time, the former PD of District Rural Development Agency (DRDA), encouraged by the then DPC, has contributed richly to the project environment in the district. On the IEC front as well as in developing a strong culture of encouraging members of SC and ST categories to join the MGNREGA, the DPC and the district team have made serious effort. Bonded labourers working in brick kilns were emancipated and were issued job cards. While the wage rate continues to be depressed, workers are happy that they do not have to migrate. In fact, many workers from small and medium enterprises (SMEs) who do not get timely payments in SMEs are returning back to villages to participate in MGNREGA works. The district has made intensive efforts to implement MGNREGA despite the fact that industrial enterprises constituted an important element of the district economy.

Deficiencies observed

The following deficiencies are observed:

(i) Worksite facilities such as shade and crèche are not available.
(ii) Inter-habitation equity is not taken care of.
(iii) There is not much of convergence with line departments.
(iv) Limitation of two works per GP is observed.
(v) Habitation-wise data of jobseekers is not available.

On the whole, the district performance with respect to transparency, equity, wage payment, monitoring and evaluation, involvement and capacity building is satisfactory.

Based on the visit of only one site close to Coimbatore city, it was observed that records are well maintained. This was a high wage pocket being very close to the city. Women only reported for work. Like in Thrissur, here also there was a clamour for more than 100 days of employment under the programme. The site was deepening of a pond which is a useful asset to the village community. Everybody had a job card. Entries matched with muster rolls. In Tamil Nadu, wage payments are by a committee on predetermined dates. The workers were satisfied with the system of wage payments.

3.4 REPORT OF NATIONAL COMMITTEE FOR MGNREGS ADMINISTRATIVE AWARDS 2010–11: DHALAI DISTRICT (TRIPURA)[4]

District profile

Dhalai District is the least populous district among the four districts (East, West, North and South Tripura) of Tripura. It is the youngest district in Tripura. More than 70% of this district is hilly and forest covered. In Dhalai District, there are five blocks, viz., Ambassa, Chawmanu, Dumburnagar, Manu and Salema. There are 130 GPs and two non-*panchayat* areas. The district occupies an area of 2,523 sq. km. It is one of the country's 250 most backward districts (out of a total of 640 districts). It is the only district in Tripura receiving the Backward Regions Grant Fund (BRGF) Programme.

According to the 2011 census, it has a population of 3.78 lakh. Near about 1.86 lakh STs and 0.51 lakh SCs and 0.98 lakh others are residing in Tripura. Dhalai is a tribal-dominated district with 57% of its population being STs and 16% SCs. It has a population density of 157 inhabitants per square kilometre and literacy rate of 86.8%. A significant percentage of population is dependent on agriculture, which requires unskilled manual work. Employment in agriculture is seasonal; however, migration of men is a common phenomenon. The total irrigated area in the district is about 1,993 hectares. The major crops cultivated in the district are paddy, jute, mesta and pineapple. The population of Dhalai consists of mostly marginal or landless farmers with very little family income. Nearly 32% of the ST population (17,705 families) are *Jhumia* families. As part of the Sixth Schedule, certain powers are shared with the Area Development Council (ADC). About 80% of the population is residing under the ADC and 20% under non-crucial area.

Performance of MGNREGS in the district

The total households registered under MGNREGS are 0.74 lakh while job card has been issued to 0.74% households, of which only 0.61 lakh job card holders have demanded employment. Near about 1.59 lakh persons have been employed and created 31.28 lakh person-days of employment. About 9.53% of SCs, 57.4% of STs and 46% women have

been provided employment. Only 6,510 households have completed 100 days out of 0.1 job-demanding households. The employment generated is very low when compared to the demand. Only 10% of households could complete 100 days of employment in spite of three backward blocks. It is noticed that the awareness levels among the wage seekers is low, even though the MGNREGS programme is being implemented for the past five years. The awareness on rights and entitlements among various stake-holders is poor in the district. The projects are proposed by the beneficiary in the GS and the same is approved by the GS/ADC.

In Jaganathpur Village Council, the team was told that the whole village had gone to a wedding celebration and was not available. Accordingly, we were taken to the shop of one Samul Das, who was available in his shop, which is adjacent to the main road and immediately accessible to any visitor. Mr Das reported that being a migrant from Bangladesh he settled down in the village and acquired the land. He and his family are assessed to be an APL family, but nevertheless are the beneficiaries of almost all development schemes, including IAY, horticulture schemes, fisheries schemes, land development schemes, MGNREGA and the like.

Mr Das is also registered under the MGNREGA and has been issued job card no. TR04001009005177. But as he did not work for a single day in the past three years, hence his card was cancelled. He, however, was successful in recovering his job card. In the interim, he proposed the construction of a bund on his agriculture land which would create a fish pond. The cost of the project is ₹1.56 lakh, estimated person-days generated are 1,336 and about 60 job card holders are reported to have received employment on an average of 22 days, though Mr Das is reported to have worked for 60 days. After the completion of the fish bund, the fisheries department has provided fingerlings free of cost. In the same village council, some of the villagers reported that community land was developed and a fish tank was constructed under NREGA and stocked with fish. Two self-help groups (SHGs) have intermittently taken a lease to harvest fish from the tank and benefitted. On an average, 70–80% of work turnout is reported to have been achieved. However, full wages (₹118) are paid to each wage seeker per day without considering the measurements or work output, though the authorities are aware that a volume of 42 cft of hard soil or 25 cft of rocky soil or 59.2 cft soft soil needs to be excavated per person per day, to earn a minimum wage of ₹118 in accordance with the approved rural SoR. It is observed that this system is practised

---

[4] This visit report has comments of V. Suresh Babu and Pradip Prabhu who visited the district. Please see the summary and theme-wise reports for comments of K.B. Saxena.

across the district with attendant questions of free riders and irregular workers remaining unanswered. The answer given by the authorities is that the present system has been in vogue from the start of the scheme and was adopted to provide wages to the wage seekers, though we are officially informed that the measurement approach is being adopted.

The officials also visited Surendrapada of the same village populated by Debarma, Reyang and Garo tribal communities. The Debarma is a predominant group in the village. Small ponds are constructed on individual paddy lands by excavating the soil and building bunds around the excavated area to form a fish pond. Nine SHGs are benefitted by leasing in land. In each SHG, there are 11 members, out of them nine members are female and two are male. The head of the SHG is a Garo and remaining members are SC Bengalis. In the village council, 70% of works are individual works and another 30% are community works. In individual land, works such as land levelling, construction of *kaccha* drain, fish ponds and plantations (bamboo, banana, mulberry and pineapple) are executed, while in community land, formation of new tanks or roads, flood control measures and soil and moisture conservation works are executed. Nurseries of bamboo and mulberry are maintained by the SHGs. Each beneficiary has 6 *kanni* of land of which paddy is cultivated in 1 *kanni*, water tank in 1 *kanni*, construction of house in 2 *kanni* and other 2 *kanni* for plantations (citrus, banana, pineapple, etc.). As observed in the previous village, on an average, 70–80% of work turnout is reported to have been achieved. However, though a volume of 42 cft of hard soil or 25 cft of rocky soil or 59.2 cft soft soil needs to be excavated per person per day, to earn a minimum wage of ₹118 in accordance with the approved rural SoR, full wages of ₹118 are paid to each wage seeker per day without considering the measurements or work output in the village too. It is also observed that usually a single work is executed under MGNREGS in a village council, at a time.

In Mogpara, the residents are Mogs, a distinct tribal community who live in separate habitations. The *jhum* land holdings of the residents of Mogpara have been recognized under the Forest Rights Act (FRA) 2006 and issued permanent *pattas* in the year 2010–11. About 28 families have been benefitted under the FRA. Another 7–8 hectare land has been assigned for protection under the Joint Forest Management Committee (JFMC). As it is also observed across all the areas visited, though MGNREGS is a demand-driven programme, most of the projects are formulated and managed by the departmental officials, with the wage seekers' involvement limited to being wage seekers and nothing more. Hence, the officials of Agriculture, Horticulture, Fisheries and Forest Departments fill in applications of the beneficiaries of assigned land under the FRA to provide banana and other plantations, hitherto under *jhum* cultivation. Presently, wage employment has been completed on the land of six FRA beneficiary families to establish banana plantation on contour bunds and pineapple plantation on the slopes. In one hectare, 12,500 pineapples are planted or 1,200 bananas are planted at a spacing of 9 × 9 ft. In 2010–11, pineapples were cultivated in 45 beneficiaries' plots. For example, in Mr Mog Kiojoy's land, pineapple was cultivated in one hectare with a total project cost of ₹180,834. The material cost was ₹78,174 and the work generated 870 person-days. In each plot, 25 wage seekers were deployed for a period of eight to nine days, to carry out land levelling and planting of pineapples which is a three-year crop.

Two issues agitated the minds of the visitors during their interaction with the village community. The first was the unevenness of wage work distribution. While Thamia Nag and Hema Mog bearing job card no. TR 04001009004026 had worked for 111 days, a few villagers who were interested in MGNREGS work were denied job cards. Accordingly, the need was recognized to undertake a massive drive to provide job cards and ration cards. A second observation was the replacement of food and vegetable crops which provided subsistence to the local people with commercial crops, whether fish farming or fruit farming, resulting in new dependencies on the market both for sale of the produce of the land and purchase of food from the market. Some of the Mog youth have resorted to head-loading of firewood to meet their daily food needs in the interim as their *jhum* lands are now covered by fruit crops which will take between 12 and 36 months to generate income.

Additionally as has been observed in the previous villages, on an average, 70–80% of work turnout is reported to have been achieved. However, in the absence of work norms for horticulture, there is no norm about the quantum of work to be performed per person per day, to earn a minimum wage of ₹118. But in accordance with the approved rural SoR, full wages of ₹118 are paid to each wage seeker per day without considering the measurements or work output, the questions of free riders and irregular workers remain unanswered.

On day two of the visit, it was decided to visit NREGA sites in Chawmanu Block. The first site visited was in the territory of the Manarchara Village

Council, where 2.0 lakh bamboo seedlings are raised on a permanent seedling raising platform. The proposal of raising bamboo seedlings under MGNREGA is not a public proposal but it was submitted by the Divisional Forest Officer (DFO) to the DPC for approval. About 495 one-year-old seedlings were distributed to the 590 beneficiaries to be planted in a spacing of 4.5 m × 4.5 m on *jhum* lands assigned to the claimants under the FRA. The forest department has not provided any forward linkage. The bamboo is harvested once in a year to make *agarbatti* and match sticks. The total cost of 2010–11 bamboo nursery projects is ₹27.81 lakh covered under MGNREGA funds. However, on a closer inquiry, the team was given to understand that the labour component in the bamboo nursery project was limited to 3% while 97% of the costs reportedly covered material cost (overhead tank, cement nursery raising platform, barbed wire and irrigation pipeline).

The next worksite visited was in the territory North Longtharai village council. The work consisted of land excavation to create a large fish pond in the lands of one Joset Chakma taken up (work order no. B1-136 dated 4 January 2011) with a cost of ₹3.89 lakh which reportedly generated 3,879 person-days of work. The project was executed by the *Gram Rozgar Sahayak* on individual lands who completed the work on 5 February 2011. Soil was excavated up to a depth of 3.5 ft over 2,400 sq. m to convert swampy land to a large fish tank. In fact, the excavated land was a cultivable land of Mr Chakma which was reduced to swampy land following the construction of PMGSY road by Hindustan Steel Corporation Limited (HSCL) without appropriate drainage. A simple culvert would have resolved the problem of drainage of the land of Mr Chakma. However, rather than providing draining to the land and correcting the damage made by HSCL, pond excavation was carried out under MGNREGS. The beneficiary lost the cultivable land and has now to depend on fish pond. The team also visited another work where land levelling was undertaken up in 6.25 *kanni* (equivalent to 1 hectare) of Mr Mringun Joy Chakma bearing job card no. TR04002010005/55.

In LaraiKarbari Para, Mr U.J. Mog was issued a *patta* for 2 acres forest land under the FRA bearing *khatian* no. 2/1 serial no. 84. However, land levelling is being carried out under MGNREGS in 3.5 acres. Details of last week payments are not known to the wage seeker due to delay in payment. As job cards are not being updated and wages are being disbursed using biometric card, illiterate wage seekers are in the dark about the actual wages earned and the amount being paid. Amana Begam (wife) and Sejim Ansari (husband) both the names are mentioned on Biometric card no. CMN 09-2041/100010072 issued by Tripura State Cooperative Bank Limited. The information prescribed to be mentioned on the worksite board is not provided on the information board hanged at the worksite. Except first-aid box, no other worksite facilities are provided.

The team also observed that in muster roll no. 20084847 and 46 whitener had been used to change the name of the beneficiary. Capacity building of stakeholders is very crucial for effective implementation of MGNREGS works. Most of the muster rolls are filled up in English which cannot be read by the members of the village community. The issue of absence of measurement and a flat wage being paid to all who report to work, irrespective of the actual work done by the wage seeker, was also observed here. The second issue which the team also observed is that the planning process under MGNREGS is very weak and as a result large sums of money is utilized to provide individual benefits to a few under the cover of giving work to wage seekers under MGNREGS. No thought has been given to the fact that MGNREGS works as a large hidden subsidy to a few individuals, while the bulk of the people provide wage labour to improve the economic conditions of a few individuals or groups.

In Sadhuram Roja Para of Makarcherra village committee, a fish pond was excavated by the Kha-Khakham SHG in the land purchased from Kalcham Chakma, one of the members, at a cost of ₹85,000. The SHG, consisting of 10 members, has utilized part of their 2nd grade loan amount of ₹3.0 lakh to purchase the land. The cost of excavation of fish pond is ₹1.19 lakh with 1,003 man-days. Three SHG members are involved in the work, viz., Chakbesing Tripuri, Thaiyarai Tripuri and Tritharam Tripuri. However, no uniformity in the quantum of work to be generated was observed while planning on the project. Though the wage rates vary from estimate to estimate (viz., ordinary soil—77 cft per person-day; hard soil—55 cft per person-day and jungle clearance—45 sq. m per person-day), the wage paid to the workers are uniform, with the attendant contradictions and contraventions which have been observed across all works.

The team also visited the bamboo plantation (it has species, viz., Dentrocalamusstrictus and local species such as Borak, Powra, Bom, Mirtinga, Makel, Rupai and Kanakkaich which are useful in the manufacture of *agarbatti* sticks, in 47 hectares over a period of three years). The details are provided in Table 3.1.

Table 3.1 Bamboo plantation cost calculations

Project period	Cost per hectare per year (₹)	Man-days generated per year per hectare
First year	13,848	66.50
Second year	5,150	40.50
Third year	3,800	38
Total	22,798	145

About 114 families have been benefitted under this project. An area of one hectare per family is considered for development planting 495 bamboo plants per acre at 4.5 m × 4.5 m.

The project implementing agency, which is the forest department, is not clear about the concept and cost incurred in the project, notwithstanding the calculations provided in Table 3.1. The wage seekers are also in the dark about their wage entitlements and the work that they have to do in the respective work. However, one observes that over time the bamboo which has been planted in the *jhum* cultivation plots will amply meet the objective of the forest department which is of removing *jhum* cultivation on the hill slopes and replacing them with forest-related species such as bamboo. This is rationalized on the ground that it would provide future income to the cultivators since bamboo could be used to make *agarbatti* sticks for selling in the market. However, the bamboo project will effectively deny the food security of the tribals as the bamboo will replace food crops on their lands under cultivation and they will have to depend on the market or on clearing forest for new *jhum* land to meet their food security needs.

In Manikpur village committee, total job cards issued is 726 out of 794 families. Job cards are not issued to every household. There is no clarity in details of job cards registered. Updation of job card register is necessary. Quorum is not maintained while conducting the GSs (either during planning MGNREGS or social audit). Not a single complaint has been registered in the complaint register. In the asset register, page no. 31, the total cost incurred is ₹225,000 (₹224,000 + contingency ₹1,000). However, the total cost is mentioned as ₹222,000. The asset register is not maintained properly. The village monitoring committee (VMC) is in place but 50% of women representation in the VMC has not been complied with. Social audit is conducted by the third party, viz., Society for Social Services Madhya Bharat chapter, Bhilai, Durg No. 034 dated 22 October 2011. The social audit report concluded that (i) cash book is not updated from 7 July 2011 to 22 October 2011 and (ii) employment register is not updated and (iii) asset and budget control registers were updated.

Affirmative action to enhance the participation of marginalized community

Overall, the district has completed 13,619 works. Majority of works executed under MGNREGS are reported to be in the category of water harvesting and water conservation (28.8%), land development (26.1%), rural connectivity (25.4%), drought proofing (8.6%), minor and micro irrigation facilities (5.8%) and flood control (0.9%).

During field visit, it is noticed that most of the MGNREGS works are executed in the individual lands though the MIS data report only 0.2% of works are executed on individual lands—a fact that is worrisome as actual data are not being updated regularly. Hence, figures on the ground are not reflected in the MIS data.

Grievance redressal mechanism

There are hardly any complaints registered in the complaint register. However, during social audit, a few issues as mentioned earlier are reported. Redressal mechanism is not effective, on the issues flagged during social audit. The awareness on complaint box, toll-free number and complaint register among the wage seekers is limited or non-existent. Wage seekers have no grievances, as they are paid full wages, irrespective of the amount of work that they have done, within the prescribed period. However, it was reported that the people considered MGNREGA as a windfall and a steady source of income in an area with very few income-generating opportunities than agriculture or migration and hence would not want to disturb a steady source of income with unnecessary grievances.

Economic benefits/land-based activities to the STs (FRA beneficiaries)

Under the Scheduled Tribes and Other Forest Dwellers (Recognition of Forest Rights) Act, 2006, 31,055 tribals were provided with forest *patta* entitlement of average land holding of 1.86 hectare which include all the *jhumia* families and other STs dependent on forests. In an effort to provide sustainable livelihoods to these beneficiaries through land-based activities, the State Government embarked on the initiative through the schemes of line departments and MGNREGA as per the choice of the beneficiaries and technical and environmental feasibility of the options.

A three-year action plan has been chalked out to cover all the beneficiaries by 2013–14 through line departments and MGNREGA schemes. Till October this year, 12,698 FRA beneficiaries have been covered and the remaining would be covered in the next two years. Out of these, 10,131 were covered under Category IV works under MGNREGA. It mainly includes land development, horticulture, fodder, bamboo and mulberry plantations and fish cultivation-related activities. Convergence with the schemes/activities of departments was also provided to ensure backward and forward linkages. All the beneficiaries are also being brought under the fold of SHGs to avail the benefits of group and individual credits and training under *Swarjayanti Gram Swarozgar Yojana* (SGSY)/National Rural Livelihood Mission (NRLM) and to sustain their livelihood options beyond the MGNREGA and other line departments' project period.

The above-mentioned efforts are made to ensure provision of annual income of at least ₹30,000 to each ST family by 2013–14 and MGNREGA shall be the most important means to achieve this. The penetration provided by the Business Correspondent Model will allow the income to reach the people without distress or difficulty which will also be a major achievement.

Notwithstanding the possibilities and achievements, serious questions remain which are as follows:

1. The first concern that the district administration must address is how to graduate from a wage for attendance approach to a wage for work approach. The current approach of wages for attendance approach is fraught with serious problems of free riding by the village elites.
2. The second concern which emerges from the present approach is the indiscipline in work management following a lack of correlation between wages paid and work done. The team was not able to decipher whether any work was planned before it is implemented or prepared later through a process of reverse correlating of wages distributed to corresponding volume of work required.
3. The third concern which needs to be addressed is the absence of measurements of work done by the individuals or groups by the mate. While attendance is shown to be taken for each shift, there are no records to show the volume of work done on a particular day or in a particular week and its correlation to the wages paid.
4. The fourth concern is how the district mediates the shift from a 'guaranteed wage programme' approach that appears to be the method that it

has adopted to a 'guaranteed wage for work performed employment programme'.
5. The fifth concern arises where the forest department in the name of convergence is using NREGS to reconvert the *jhum* lands where the tribals grew their food and vegetable crops into fruit orchards or bamboo plantations whose products will eventually be sold in the market. What will be the long-term impact of the conversion of *jhum* lands which provided a vast variety of crops and food security to plantations which will provide produce for the market? Whether this model will be sustainable in the long run remains a matter of concern.
6. The sixth concern is whether the traditional model of relative self-sufficiency based on subsistence self-cultivation will survive the model of market-driven surplus production and sale being promoted in the name of NREGS. Will it result in newer lands being brought under *jhum* by forest clearing as the tribal people fight the insecurity of the market with the security of practices which have evolved over centuries?
7. The seventh concern is the potential loss of the gene pool of crops grown on the *jhum* lands now being converted into fruit orchards or bamboo plantations. The elimination of this rich gene pool which has been preserved for centuries remains an ever-present threat following the systematic takeover by the forest department of *jhum* lands whose rights have been conferred to the tribals.
8. The eighth concern is how the tribal communities will manage the transition from being a self-sufficient subsistence economy, which they have built over generations, to a market-driven 'surplus economy'. Is the dependence on the market an intended goal or an unintended impact? This question has to be addressed by the district administration which is spearheading a 'wage employment programme' in convergence with other agencies who have different objectives such as unstated objective of the forest department, examining which is a long-term question that needs to be answered.
9. The ninth concern is that MGNREGS is currently accelerating the passage of the tribal community from a subsistence economy to a market-dependent surplus economy, without their prior informed consent. Will this transition be beneficial to the tribal people, or will it result in societal and cultural conflict or change which the community will have to manage willingly or unwillingly or will it be a burden that the scheme has unwittingly left for the next generation to handle? These questions need to be addressed.

Box 3.1 Payment of wages through business correspondence model*

The difficult terrain, poor infrastructure, inadequate road connectivity and 80% of the land being under forest make it difficult for various citizen services to reach to the poor who reside in the far flung remote villages of the district. In order to bring transparency and plug any leakages of funds, the payments to the wage seekers are directly paid into their bank accounts. However, due to lack of expansion of bank branches in a district, where there are only 25 branches (covering about 130 villages or 1,067 habitations), the payment of wages through bank's branches has turned out to be expensive and time consuming and has brought more hardship to the poor tribals living in the remote locations (30–40 km away from their houses). The wage seeker has to spend about ₹50 to ₹100 for their journey to collect their wages from the concerned bank branch. It is estimated that this transaction results in a loss of about ₹8.16 crore annually to the wage seekers of Dhalai. Even worse, many a time the wage seeker is not able to draw his wages due to long queues, holidays and other delays. This high transaction cost necessitated a technological intervention not only to ensure payment of wages nearer to the door step of the wage seeker but also to make it more frequent and regular every month.

The business correspondence model was thus taken up as a technological intervention by the district administration to bring down the transaction cost for wage payment and provide banking services to the doorstep of the worker. For providing the services under the this model two banks, namely, Tripura Gramin Bank and Tripura State Cooperative Bank with 16 numbers of branches covering about 99 GPs/VSs and about 737 habitations were selected. The State Government and NABARD played a key role in getting the banks adopt the business correspondence model to deliver its services by incurring a cost of ₹50 each for every job card holder. Table 3.2 shows the current status of the implementation of the business correspondence model in the district.

Table 3.2 Status of implementation of business correspondence model

	No. of GPs/VCs to be covered	No. GP/ADC villages covered	No. of registered job card holders	No. of enrolment completed	No. of smart card issued	No. of smart cards distributed	No. of villages with payment started through business correspondence model	No. of left-out households
TGB	50	50	24,995	24,510	23,778	23,778	50	485
TSCB	49	49	27,471	26,160	25,249	25,249	49	1,311
SBI	12	6	6,778	3,860	0	0	0	2,918
UBI	19	19	10,788	10,189	2,181	52	0	599
Total	**130**	**124**	**70,032**	**64,719**	**51,208**	**49,079**	**99**	**5,313**

It is thus evident from Table 3.2 that the business correspondence model is currently being implemented in 99 GPs/VCs and through this model about 75% of the job card holders and almost every remote location are currently being served. The district administration plans to reach the remaining GPs/VCs through national banks such as State Bank of India and Union Bank of India which also have branches in the district by December 2011.

The business correspondence model, despite the hilly terrain in the district and sprouts of insurgency-related activities, has been very successful in the district. The business correspondence model disburses a total of about ₹60 crore in a year for MGNREGA wage payment. Most of the transactions are done on *haat* days where the wage seekers are able to withdraw money and do their weekly shopping in the market. This aggregation thus reduces the time and cost for the wage seekers and makes it extremely convenient for them, while for the business correspondents it reduces the transportation and logistical costs. The wages are paid on time and the leakages in wage payment are effectively reduced through the business correspondence model. In near future, with proper education and awareness campaign, the model can be expanded into providing other financial services to the poor such as access to credit, insurance, etc.

*This is based on the handout provided by the district administration.

Box 3.2 MGNREGS and its impact on insurgency*

The porous borders in the three blocks of district have made the population in the border villages (34) very susceptible to the tribal insurgency of groups such as National Liberation Front of Tripura (NLFT) and All Tripura Tiger Force (ATTF). Though the ideology of insurgency has now reduced to mere extortion, every year the incidences such as kidnapping, killings and ambush of the security personnel were on the rise till 2006–07. MGNREG programme was introduced in Dhalai in 2006–07 as a Phase I district for providing 100 days of wage employment. Since then an average of 80–90 person-days has been provided to the wage seekers every year. It has been more in the border blocks of Chawmanu, Dumburnagar and Ambassa. In Chawmanu which has 14 border villages, all the job card holders were provided with 100 days of employment including the rural tribal youths. This has ensured no further recruitments to the cadre of insurgent groups which were already getting weakened.

According to an intelligence report, the strength of NLFT cadres has remained at 150–200 since 2009–10 and many insurgents are likely to surrender after seeing the brighter side of life. Most of the surrendered militants who reside in the villages are job card holders and have got 90–100 average man-days work. In Dhalai, out of 1,726 surrendered militants, 1,509 still reside in their villages and 1,469 are the MGNREGS job card holders. In addition to the one-time surrender package by the government, MGNREGS has ensured providing secure livelihood options to the persons (surrendered militants) who were detached from other traditional livelihoods and land-based activities on their return.

*This is based on the handout provided by the district administration.

3.5 REPORT OF NATIONAL COMMITTEE FOR MGNREGS ADMINISTRATIVE AWARDS 2010–11: DHAMTARI DISTRICT (CHHATTISGARH)[5]

Observations

In Dhamtari District, payment of ₹8–10 crore for materials was pending across several blocks and *panchayat*s of the district for the past one year because of audit objections. As a result of which NREGS works had been halted in several of them. This exposed lack of adequate monitoring for timely intervention. It also showed that field inspections and supervision were lacking. If these were undertaken, these were poor in quality.

Software for tracking the movement of muster roll to determine the delay in processing, measurement, completion and payment was introduced by the District Magistrate. A register was maintained at the district level for this purpose. Still there was huge delay in submission and verification of muster roll which the software system could not detect. Nearly 17 GRSs had been dismissed for delay in submission of muster roll. Around three BDOs had been penalized to pay a fine of ₹1,000 for the delay.

In Kamarpara, a habitation of 14 households of the Kamars (STs) adjacent to the reserve forest area

[5] Summary points of K.B. Saxena's visit to the district.

and whose residents are among the poorest people in Dhamtari District, the team encountered the abject poverty and utter helpless situation they were in. While they had job cards, the forest department had just not engaged them in its works or allowed NREGS work to be taken up in their *para* (habitation) for the past several years. The GP did not keep them informed about work in the area or allocated work in their *para*. The *panch* and *sarpanch* of the GP asked them to go back when they went there seeking work ('*Panchayat waale bataate nahin hain; Waapis kar dete hain, panch, sarpanch*' [*Panchayat* people do not tell us about work and direct us to go back]). Their land *patta* applications were also pending with the forest department. However, during the past five months, they had been able to get some work.

In the district, the team got information that masons (skilled category of workers) were not only drawing the prevailing market-rate wages which were higher than stipulated under NREGS but also working for 200 days. Their wages were being booked under material component and therefore did not attract notice.

In this Phase I district, across several villages of different blocks and *panchayat*s, job cards had been taken away by officials since June 2011 under the pretext of renewal. Villagers hence could not demand work.

In earthen/field/rural connectivity road works, it was observed in at least three places (Dhamtari and Vizianagaram Districts, for instance) that earth (the good top soil) was being excavated from the adjacent fields of farmers (possibly tribals). Earth could be taken from the waste land, which was easily available, than from the farmer's field, as it would get destroyed. It takes a long time for top soil to be formed which contains vital nutrients within it. This sensitivity in implementing officials was lacking.

The watershed principle was largely not being adhered to in taking up of water development schemes, thereby leading to suboptimal benefits of water bodies and land development activities. In Amlipaar village, Bhotapa GP (Dhamtari District), there was a need to develop plantations on the ridge forming the high ground of the local tiny watersheds. Water had to be arrested in higher reaches. Also, an area plan had to be made.

In Singur GP (Dhamtari), the team saw huge fencing (near Birjhuli/Birmuli road) of cemented poles on one side of the main road to protect forests from grazing by cattle (reared by the villagers) though there was no village in the immediate vicinity. It could not be verified whether NREGS funds were used for this fencing.

Across the districts, awareness about filing claims for forest land (*patta*) under the FRA was very low. It was learnt that in some villages in Keonjhar, Dhamtari and Sarguja Districts, a lot of tribals had not even filed their claims because they were not aware of the law and procedure to put up a claim before the FRA Committee. The district administration should look into it. In several places where claims had been filed, these had been pending for years. In several cases there was a drastic reduction in the allocation of land vis-à-vis the claim submitted. Additionally, a good number of claims were rejected which the petitioner had not re-submitted for review. Officials should have intervened to seek cooperation of the forest department in solving people's problems.

In Gohan *nala* village of Munaikera *panchayat* (Nagori Block, Dhamtari), three separate ponds, adjacent to each other, below the slope of a forest and at some distance from the village were constructed through *shramdaan*. It was on the land of Patels, the influential class. However, these too were technically flawed as rainwater spilled over in the monsoons. Adequate compacting of the foreshore (*medh*) had not been done, leading to cracks in walls and spillage of water. No channels (*naali*) had been constructed to take water to the fields. Due to scarcity, the water was used only for drinking purposes, both cattle and people. It seemed strange that despite construction of so many ponds, no irrigation water was available to villagers.

3.6 REPORT OF NATIONAL COMMITTEE FOR MGNREGS ADMINISTRATIVE AWARDS 2010–11: DHAR DISTRICT (MADHYA PRADESH)[6]

District profile

Dhar District (17.40 lakh population) comprises a total of 13 blocks, including 12 tribal blocks. It has a total of 761 GPs and 1,474 villages. It has a low literacy rate of 52.4%. SCs and STs constitute nearly 60% of the total population (SCs: 6.9% and STs: 53.01%). Opportunities of livelihood are very limited. The major occupation of the people is agriculture and daily wage labour. It has an agrarian single-crop economy, shifting from forest to agriculture. There is high seasonal migration in the district.

Performance of MGNREGS in the district

General performance was observed to be quite satisfactory. Under MGNREGA, traditional forest dwellers [who were allotted *pattas* for their land holdings under the Scheduled Tribe (ST) and Other Forest Dwellers (Forest Rights) Act 2008] were systematically targeted by the district administration in a focussed manner through a process of 'Net Planning'.

The process involved an initial base-line survey to identify block- and GP-specific opportunities for land development, horticulture plantations and farm bunding works, besides excavation of wells in convergence with the Kapildhara scheme of the Government of Madhya Pradesh. A comprehensive format with 42 columns was designed to capture complete information about land development needs, and scope for convergence with sericulture, horticulture, fisheries, canal irrigation (Sahastradhara) and well-irrigation (Kapildhara) schemes of the State.

Affirmative action to enhance the participation of marginalized community

In the villages identified for field visits, 70–80% of the wage seekers who completed 100 days of employment under MGNREGA in the year 2010–11 were STs.

Good practices

Besides the planning system, it was observed that a massive change in the cropping pattern from traditional millets to economically remunerative crops such as vegetables and fruit orchards was underway without entirely giving up cultivation of cereals and millets for home consumption by the tribal farmers.

[6] This visit report has comments of Hemnath Rao with inputs of Nilay Ranjan who visited the district.

Table 3.3 Team observations against outcome indicators of MGNREGA programme

Outcome indicator	Achievement	Sources of information	Observation of award team
Land allocation to beneficiaries under the FRA	Allotment of *patta*s	Information given by villagers in the GS; agriculture department	A good initiative. In the 12 GPs and three blocks visited, people had received land *patta*s.
MGNREGA works on the land of FRA beneficiaries	23,000	MGNREGA MIS	Good work as people have started cultivation of land. In few villages, the agriculture department was also providing inputs and other facilities such as vegetable kit, seeds, drip irrigation and tools.
Provision of employment	142 lakh man-days of wage employment	MGNREGS MIS, departmental information	On an average, people received 50–60 days of employment in the current year (2011–12) and 70 days in the year 2010–11. This was verified with job card entries, muster rolls and also with MIS. District officials also monitor this at the block level.
Area under double crop cultivation	Increased by 2,000 hectares	Land revenue department	*Patta* owners have started cultivation on their land, which was not in use earlier. Due to water conservation works also, land productivity has improved.
Irrigated land	Increased by 20,000 hectares	Land revenue department	*Patta* owners have brought more/new land under cultivation with the availability of irrigation facilities.
Area covered under drip irrigation	500 hectares	Agriculture/horticulture department	This is a good example of convergence with the agriculture department. Land developed under MGNREGA is being used by the agriculture department to provide agriculture and irrigation-related subsidies and training.
Migration	Has stopped to a large extent	GS	There is a decline in migration due to better opportunities and higher wages in rural areas. Earlier a large group of workers migrated to Gujarat. Now around 40% people prefer to stay in the village.

In one particular village (Bhil Bharkeda), the introduction of bottle gourd (*kaddu*) has enhanced the farmers' income threefold. The most striking feature was that in a valley 200 metres below the land surface, a small group of five tribal families was identified for development of their land as well as excavation of wells under MGNREGA. A significant outcome from the targeted provision of MGNREGA works to tribal farmers converged with the Kapildhara wells has been the sustainability of livelihoods for tribal farmers.

Other observations

The Chief Executive Officer (CEO) of the *Zila Parishad* and his team of professionals were observed to be the driving force behind the programme implementation. The project team was found to be working as a cohesive team under his leadership.

Table 3.3 records the observations of the team against the outcome indicators of the MGNREGA programme.

3.7 REPORT OF NATIONAL COMMITTEE FOR MGNREGS ADMINISTRATIVE AWARDS 2010–11: KEONJHAR DISTRICT (ODISHA)[7]

Observations

Three blocks, namely, Patna, Saharpada and Jhumpura were visited on 18th and 19th of December 2011. In the block headquarters, records, data and reports were inspected and interactions with the POs

[7] This report has comments of Bhagirath Panda who visited the district. Please see the summary and theme-wise reports for comments of K.B. Saxena.

and other MGNREGS functionaries were held. The programme in terms of equity, inclusion, capacity building, monitoring and evaluation, grievance redress, transparency and efficiency and conformation to MGNREGS norms and guidelines was evaluated. In the field, GP offices (of Palanaghati, Basantapur, Malapada, Kandeipasi and Bayakumutia) and worksites/villages at Kenduapada, Silda, Godhirampada and Mundula were visited.

Mundula village

Mundula village is basically inhabited by a tribe called Bhuiyans. Interaction with the villagers and wage seekers in this village brought out the following:

1. *Gram sabha* (*Palli sabha*) has not been convened for the last one year.
2. There is delay in payments which exceed two months.
3. There is demand for work but work has not been given.
4. GRS has not been imparted any training.

Basantpur GP

Inspection of records and documents in Basantapur GP and interaction with wage seekers/villagers there brought out the following:
Plus points: (a) Records were kept properly and (b) *Palli sabha* was convened twice during 2010–11.
Deficiencies: (a) There is exclusion of beneficiaries. Jobseekers Bhagirathi Mahanta and Bidesi Penthei were not given work although they had demanded work. The GP functionary could not give any satisfactory answer and acknowledged this exclusion. (b) In many instances, it was found that the entries in job cards were not updated.

Malapada GP

Plus points: (a) Most registers were maintained properly. (b) *Gram sabha* was convened regularly. (c) Complaint redressal system exists.
Deficiencies: (a) The GRS remained absent deliberately during the time of inspection. (b) Cash voucher could not be produced. (c) Interaction with jobseekers confirmed delay in payment in two cases exceeding one month.

Saharapada Block

Poor record keeping is observed. Some of the vouchers are without voucher number, date and signature of the accountant, BDO and ABDO.

Silda village and worksite (road construction from Mundasahi to Silda temple)

The team interacted with the jobseekers and checked the job cards of Masuri Munda, Tima Nayak and Pratp Munda and in all cases found delayed payment up to one and half months.

Improvement of Kusumtangar pond in Godhirampada village in Palanghati GP of Patna Block

This work has realized convergence effectively. This village is situated on the foothills and about 80 acres of land used to get silted because of the heavy water flow from the hills during the rains. In collaboration with one NGO called WOSCA, the MGNREGS work has very effectively checked siltation and created permanent water bodies by building scientific channels. By now it has made 20 acres of land cultivable. This is an innovation.

Overall observations (actionable points)

Inclusion: The district suffers from exclusion in NREGS works. The registration of demand process is not effective. *Mobilization:* Poor. There has not been any effective mobilization of the poor tribal jobseekers to demand and get work. *Monitoring and evaluation:* Poor. *Capacity building of field functionaries:* Needs much improvement. The weakest functionary in this respect happens to be the GRS. *Rajiv Gandhi Seva Kendra and MGNREGS:* Vouchers in this programme are not properly procured. *Record keeping:* By and large, good.

3.8 REPORT OF NATIONAL COMMITTEE FOR MGNREGS ADMINISTRATIVE AWARDS 2010–11: KHARGAON DISTRICT (MADHYA PRADESH)[8]

District profile

Khargaon District is divided into five blocks, nine *tehsil*s, 600 GPs and 1,407 villages. It has tribal dominant areas and scores very low on general development indicators of literacy and health. Livelihood opportunities are limited and by and large it is a single-cropped area. Migration has traditionally been high but declining in recent years.

Performance of MGNREGS in the district

The focus of the visit was to study the revival of the Ramkola River, benefitting 11 villages of eight GPs, which was highlighted as an important achievement of the district MGNREGA team. Ramkola River, about 15.5 km in length, is a tributary to Hathni River which is a further tributary to Narma.

---

[8] This visit report has comments of Hemnath Rao with inputs of Nilay Ranjan who visited the district.

In the four GPs (Ubadi, Likhy, Ichapur and Khargone) of Khargone Block visited by the team, the level of participation of wage seekers in the MGNREGA was observed to be quite low. Also, the team learnt that revival of dried-up rivers and river beds was, in fact, a State-level initiative, which was being sought to be achieved through convergence with MGNREGS.

To revive the river, water conservation projects such as construction of contour bunds, check dams, gully plugs and related works were undertaken. Desilting of the river bed had led to improvement in net sown area. However, district officials were not aware about ridge-to-valley concept, which was not considered either during planning or during execution.

Affirmative action to enhance the participation of marginalized community

There was no significant effort to increase participation of marginalized sections nor was there evidence of any IEC work carried out in the two blocks. While some farmers in each of the three GPs (along the Ramkola River), namely, Ubadi, Likhy and Ichapur expressed satisfaction with improved net sown area following revival of the river, the benefits seemed to have accrued only to a small group of farmers whose land is drained by the river. There was no particular focus on small and marginal farmers. In fact, most of the farmers in near-the-river-side-area GPs are from upper castes having substantial land holdings.

In Itivardi village which was visited in the late hours of the evening, it was mentioned that only one SC farmer had been assigned a piece of land by the government, but even that single holding had not been developed under MGNREGS.

In Ubadi village, an upstream of Ramkola River, out of 50 households who had completed 100 days work, only one person belonged to the SC category. Similarly, in the downstream village of Likhy, a large number of pipelines have been laid for transfer of water from the river-fed tank, but the benefits have been cornered by a very small section of the farming community.

Grievance redressal mechanism

Low level of awareness of provisions of the scheme implied that grievances were hardly brought to the notice of the project staff. During an interactive session with the job card holders, some complained that machines were used for laying the pipelines. The team could not conclusively verify the same, as a somewhat tense situation began to develop during the discussions.

Revival of Ramkola River and quality of assets

Since revival of small rivers and rivulets is actually a State-sponsored/level initiative, it would *not be fair* to describe the project (revival of Ramkola River) as an innovation. It must be said to the credit of the district administration, however, that the project was pursued with single-minded devotion, though the benefits have not percolated equitably across the rural communities. Overall, implementation of the scheme in the district left much to be desired.

The assets (check dams, contour trenches, earthen bunds, etc.) created were observed to be of average quality.

Other observations

Table 3.4 mentions observations of the visiting team on outcome indicators and achievements claimed by the district MGNREGS team.

Table 3.4 **Visiting team observations versus achievements claimed by MGNREGS team**

Outcome indicator	Achievement	Sources of information	Observation of award team
Increase in annual flow of the river	Flow of water had increased by two months	Information given by villagers in GS, Pidhi Jal Sanwad, agriculture department	No evidence was available during field visit. In fact, the river bed was dry. However, few villagers in Ichapur did mention that flow has increased.
Increase in underground water table	Risen by 2 metres	Public Health Engineering Department	People are still facing water scarcity in villages.
Employment generation	2.95 lakh man-days of wage employment	MGNREGS MIS, departmental information	About 50% people in each GP still need employment. High unemployment in rural areas still persists.

(Continued)

(Continued)

Outcome indicator	Achievement	Sources of information	Observation of award team
Increase in area under double crop cultivation	Increased by 569 hectares	Land revenue department	Only some small and marginal farmers who are getting benefit under the Agriculture Technology Management Agency (ATMA) scheme have started double cropping.
Increase in land under irrigation	Increased by 746 hectares	Land revenue department	No evidence was available during the field visit.
Area brought under afforestation/fodder cultivation	41 hectares	Progress reports/ forest department	No evidence was available during the field visit.
Area covered under drip irrigation	247 hectares	Agriculture/ horticulture department(s)	This was not linked to MGNREGA.
Decrease in migration	Has stopped to a large extent	GS	There is a decline in migration due to better opportunities and higher wages in rural areas.
Sustainability of assets	Formation of user groups and their strengthening through trainings	GP/block *panchayat* reports	No evidence was available during the field visit.

3.9 REPORT OF NATIONAL COMMITTEE FOR MGNREGS ADMINISTRATIVE AWARDS 2010–11: MALKANGIRI DISTRICT (ODISHA)[9]

Located at the tip of Odisha, Malkangiri, a tribal district, is nearly 700 km away from the State capital (Bhubaneshwar). The population is spread out both in the plains and hills. It is among the Left Wing Extremism (LWE)-affected districts in the country.

It was the District Collector's initiative to provide MGNREGS to the people here, given that this was not the case earlier. In the last two years, efforts have been made to reach out to people living in hilly pockets and interior areas along with enhancing MGNREGS provisioning in the district as a whole.

A challenge of undertaking an assessment in such places is that it takes many hours to travel and further more in being able to meet the communities who live in the hilly areas. This team member focussed on visiting such areas, as this is where the LWE has a base and development effort not reaching them has been seen as the primary cause for its presence and support in the community.

The district is yet to target provisioning of 100 days of employment although it has scaled up

MGNREGS. Unless some concerted efforts are made and some flexibility allowed, it would not be possible to serve these remote areas and ensure efficient delivery of developmental efforts/schemes. The type of works taken up in the hill areas must allow incorporating additional activities. Due to non-communication with the forest department, the possibilities of works that could be undertaken under MGNREGS in these forest-dotted areas have not come up for consideration.

One important activity in the plain areas is horticulture. Plantations of mango have been taken up. Here they have done a good job of fencing and water provisioning, including storage and application. While it is possible to take up such works extensively in the plain areas where water is easily available, the real challenge is figuring out what can/must be done for communities in the hill-top areas. Creative and new ideas must be conceived, otherwise MGNREGS in the district will seem impressive but not really be reaching to the most-needy areas. It will also lead to opposition of the programme by the (needy) people for this reason.

A good measure has been the issuing of new job cards. As the district has only two government banks, payment delays are both long and inevitable. While they have adopted e-muster roll, it takes considerable time for the field staff to travel from remote areas to distant offices. There is a need to adopt variations in the approach to management

[9] This visit report has comments of K.S. Gopal who visited the district.

and deliverance of MGNREGS factoring in specificities of terrain and distances.

Road widening has been taken up extensively and there is a need to ensure that other works (than horticulture) also receive MGNREGS investment. This team member felt that we need to look at hill-based tribal areas differently in terms of costs, personnel, community participation and works under MGNREGS. Thrusting what has worked in the plain areas to such places (on the pretext of uniformity) is the biggest challenge that is not being addressed by the district, possibly because this would require clearance from the headquarters (in Bhubaneshwar).

The district has a Collector who is enthused about working hard. However, it is felt that the quality of the subordinate manpower be enhanced and it should also be motivated (as most personnel see it as punishment posting). The temporarily appointed field staff or their seniors should also be allowed some say on how the hill areas (or for that matter, plain areas) can be served better.

NGOs are being involved in certain activities especially in social audit. But as stated earlier, MGNREGS needs to have a different approach and offer, in order to facilitate the available field staff perform and deliver better. This is the basic reason why community enthusiasm was rarely observed.

In some works, say those by the horticulture department, a good synergy with other line departments was observed. However, the sad part was that the forest department, the biggest player, was not involved in MGNREGS in any manner. At best, the team saw some work on the forest lands which were given from revenue forest lands rather than reserve forest lands of the forest department which are largely in the hill areas.

Malkangiri deserves attention but the systems and processes in place are not able to deliver MGNREGS.

3.10 REPORT OF NATIONAL COMMITTEE FOR MGNREGS ADMINISTRATIVE AWARDS 2010–11: NALANDA DISTRICT (BIHAR)[10]

District profile

Popularly known as Biharsharif, Nalanda is an agriculture-dominant district. With a population of nearly 28.72 lakh, it comprises 20 blocks and 249 GPs. The population of SCs is around 66.4% and

[10] This report has comments of Hemnath Rao and V. Suresh Babu who visited the district.

that of STs around 20%. There are nearly 3.40 lakh BPL families.

Dryland agriculture is the main occupation in the district. Major crops cultivated during *kharif* are paddy, potato and onion, while during *rabi*, vegetables and potato are cultivated. The net sown area is 1.82 lakh hectares with a cropping intensity of 3,398. About 50% of the land is cultivated by the leased-in farmers. Land holding among the farming community varies from 0.5 acre to 7 acres. Among the SC farmers, land holding is meagre. The major industries in the district are of handloom and small and medium enterprises. Since Nalanda is a famous tourist destination, tourism plays a vital role in its economy.

Performance of MGNREGS in the district

It would not be fair to compare the quality of programme implementation in Nalanda District with the progress seen in other States where these processes have attained higher levels of maturity.

While the district administration had made considerable effort in enhancing awareness on wage seekers' rights as well as obligations of the GPs under the MGNREGA, awareness levels among wage seekers on their rights and entitlements were observed to be very low.

Issuing of job cards picked up momentum in recent years. About 3.98 lakh job cards have been issued so far. Employment provided increased from 38.80 lakh man-days during 2009–10 to 45.66 lakh man-days in 2010–11 (18% increase). The share of women's participation in the total person-days work provided was around 39%. The share of the SC community was 52%. On an average, only 10–12 days of employment per household was provided in the district irrespective of the category of wage seeker SC, ST and others.

The team was informed that the demand for MGNREGS had increased due to IEC activity. However, it was observed that the programme is still supply driven. There is a huge demand for employment in the district which is unmet by the administration. It was observed that during the lean employment season, landless agricultural labourers migrate to Patna (State Capital) and other neighbouring States.

The quality of record keeping (noticed in Chandi and Islampur Blocks) was generally poor and most of the MGNREGS registers were not available at the GP office. However, it was not possible to investigate the process in detail on account of a strike call given by the GRSs/Secretaries of GPs at the time of the team's field visit.

Except *Ahar* and *Pyne* water harvesting (tanks/ponds), irrigation drainage channels (repair and desilting), drought proofing (planting of trees along canal banks and plantation blocks) and rural connectivity, other category works were limited. As per work norms, men had to generate 80 cft and women 68 cft of work per day to earn their minimum wage of ₹144. However, it was observed that single measurement was recorded in the measurement book on completion of work and full wages paid to every person attending work.

Works sanctioned during previous years were being executed during the current year (2011–12) without revised budget. There was a need to get approval for the revised budget.

There was a one-month delay in wage disbursement. Since none of the job cards was updated, it was difficult to verify the person-days completed by the concerned wage seekers. In Islampur, the wage seekers informed that the job cards were kept with the GRS throughout the year and distributed a day before the arrival of the team. It was also told that wages were paid by the contractor and later withdrawn from their post office or bank account.

In Dhamoli village, it was informed that wage seekers formed a group of 8–10 members and worked under MGNREGS. Mates are paid ₹10 per day as additional payment for implementing and monitoring. The market wage rate has increased due to MGNREGS. In case of men the raise was from ₹80 to ₹150, while for women it was from ₹50 to ₹120 per day, during peak agricultural operations.

Affirmative action to enhance the participation of marginalized community

While scope exists for better focus on inclusion of members of SCs and STs, there was evidence of efforts made by project functionaries to enrol all landless families under MGNREGS on a priority basis. However, there was no emphasis on developing individual land holdings of STs and SCs. It was found that the district administration had not executed any works under Category IV as the land holdings were very small.

The nature of works selected under MGNREGS largely benefitted these communities. Most of the SC, BPL, small and marginal farmers had benefitted from the *Ahar* and *Pyne* (irrigation or water storage structures) surrounding their cultivable areas (*khand*). Due to these structures, the water table has increased by 40–50 feet in plains and by 20 feet in hilly terrains.

It was informed by the block administration that they had distributed three cents of land to SC landless agriculture labourers which was confirmed by a few wage seekers who had obtained the assigned land.

Grievance redressal mechanism

The GP and block had not received any complaints during last three years (2009–12). Village community was not aware of the toll-free number. The frequency of conducting social audit had increased from 1 during 2008–09 to three during 2011–12. However, this audit had not recorded any shortcoming. One complaint was received from a farmer stating that under MGNREGS his farmland was being dug without (his) prior permission. This was found to be a case of an encroached *Pyne* area.

Good practices

The *Ahar Pyne* system, which was the traditional source of irrigation of south Bihar, had declined over the years as most of them had been encroached upon by the landlords, leading to high run-off, flood and drought. As a result, there was a switch from use of surface water to exploiting underground water.

Pyne is the local name for the traditional irrigation channels, which are of various sizes. While the small ones originate in *Ahar*s and carrying their water to cultivable land plots, the larger ones have their origins in rivers from where water is diverted through channels by erecting embankments along the river beds. This irrigation channel system was dealt a death-blow under the nineteenth-century British colonial regime. Post-independence follow-up was hardly better.

In 2006, after the launch of MGNREGS, it provided a great opportunity to re-excavate these *Ahar*s and *Pyne*s. Hundreds of kilometres of *Pyne*s were renovated to rejuvenate the irrigation facility in the district, identified as a priority area by the community. As a result, 482 *Pyne*s were restored (in 2010–11) in Nalanda District and within three years of implementation, irrigation coverage had increased significantly by 27,600 hectares.

Improved irrigation facilities revolutionized agriculture opportunities in the region resulting in increased crop intensity and diversity. Drought spell hardly affected the *kharif* crop due to this initiative. In the process of reviving this traditional system of water management in the district, two purposes have been achieved:

1. An increase in the net sown irrigated area in the GPs visited thereby instilling confidence among farmers, particularly small and marginal ones, enhancing cropping intensity and farming incomes.
2. Migration has reduced as more and more landless labourers are seeking to take land on lease at the rate of ₹5,000 to 6,000 per *bigha* and engage themselves in active agricultural operations besides participation in MGNREGS.

The other significant achievements of reviving the traditional system are as follows:

- Increase in recharge capacity of ground water,
- Increase in availability of water during *rabi* cropping season (December to January),
- Water storage capacity had increased from 1.57 lakh m³ to 37.14 lakh m³ in the year 2009–10,
- Cropping intensity and cropping pattern had changed and reduced flooding of cultivable area and
- District administration could save ₹10 crore which was usually spent towards subsidy for diesel.

A good practice observed was to avoid parking of funds, delay in funds transfer and to increase availability and access to funds. The State Government has initiated the Central Planning Scheme and Monitoring System (CPSMS) on a pilot basis in Islampur Block.

Though no systematic effort was made to affect convergence of MGNREGS with SGSY, it was found that most wage seekers, who participated in the MGNREGS, developed the confidence to join the SHGs which were involved in culturing mushrooms which is emerging as a major income-generating activity in the villages of the district. This combination has further helped in checking migration and also contributed to their active participation in the GSs.

Other observations

A sense of commitment and confidence was evident in the district project team despite the fact that the Assistant Programme Officers were contract employees. The district team has shared understanding of the potential benefits that can flow to the landless poor as well as small and marginal farmers through MGNREGS works. The team had succeeded in reviving the traditional water management system in the district.

3.11 REPORT OF NATIONAL COMMITTEE FOR MGNREGS ADMINISTRATIVE AWARDS 2010–11: NANDED DISTRICT (MAHARASHTRA)[11]

District profile

Nanded, which falls in Marathwada region, is one of the backward districts of Maharashtra. Comprising nine *taluka*s (Nanded, Hadgaon, Kinwat, Bhokar,

[11] This report has observations of V. Suresh Babu and Hemnath Rao who visited the district.

Billoli, Degloor, Mukhed, Kandhar and Loha), it is predominantly rural (98%). Situated in the Deccan Plateau, the southern part of the district has light and barren land. About 8.3% of the district's geographical area is under forest cover.

It has a predominantly agrarian economy. Majority of its population is engaged in agricultural activities. There is little industrialization, and existing industries are agriculture based (cotton, banana and food processing). The major crops cultivated are *jowar*, cotton, *bajra*, wheat, sugarcane and banana. According to the 2011 census, Nanded has a population of 55 lakh and a high literacy rate of 76.94% (as compared to 64.87% of Maharashtra). About 17.3% of the population is from the SC community while 8.8% from the ST community.

Performance of MGNREGS in the district

The implementation of MGNREGS in the district generally bore vestigial influence of the erstwhile Maharashtra State Rural Employment Guarantee Scheme (EGS). There was clearly a lag in the understanding of the spirit of this programme and the mindset of project functionaries seemed to be still dominated by the manner in which relief works were (earlier) implemented.

Against this background, the DPC had made a significant contribution to focus the efforts of the project team on developing sustainable assets that can promote livelihood security. The efforts have yielded positive results in the area of water conservation.

About 3.47 lakh households have been issued MGNREGS job cards, of which SCs constitute 18% and STs 9%. As per the MIS data (on 27 January 2012), during 2010–11, a total of 30.65 lakh mandays were generated in which the share of SCs was 16%, the share of STs was 9% and the share of women was 47%.

Keeping in mind the total number of job cards issued to these categories, the person-days generated per household among SCs was a paltry eight days and among STs nine days; combined (SC and ST) it was only nine days. This indicates that either there is a huge unmet demand or the real job card seekers are very limited (against the total number of SC and ST households issued job cards).

The quality of record keeping was poor in almost all the blocks visited (Ardhapur, Loha, Kandhar and Mukhed) with even basic muster rolls not being signed by wage seekers. However, all registers were in place, though without updation. The work-done register was not updated after 2009–10. In none of the villages visited were the job cards updated.

It was also observed in a few GPs that job cards were not issued in continuous serial numbers. For example, in Chidgiri GP, job cards with serial numbers 295, 404–412 and 414–499 were missing. The last job card number registered in the job card issue register did not tally with the number of households issued job card in the MIS data. (On the website, the last job card number is generally considered as the total number of job cards issued.)

The shelf of works approved during 2009–10 was executed late, during 2010–11. Revised approval of their estimates was not found in any of the GPs. In Mahur Block, MGNREGS works were being executed simultaneously by the GP, forest department, agriculture department and minor irrigation department. It was also observed that none of the MGNREGS work records executed by line departments was available with either the GP or block *panchayat*, which should be the case. At each worksite, hardly 20–40 wage seekers were found.

There was considerable delay in disbursement of wages, ranging from one to one-and-a-half months. The major reason was observed to be at the level of GRS and JE, respectively. The GRS waited for one month to submit muster rolls of four weeks together, while the JE took one to four weeks to measure the work done by the wage seekers. For instance, in Shekapur, wages had not been paid since September as the GRS was waiting to submit 4–5 muster rolls together. Further, the delay was also due to lack of funds.

In some cases, there was a delay of two to three months in wage disbursement. One of the *sarpanch*s (who has held this post continuously for past 19 years and is also a recipient of *Nirmal Gram Puraskar*) mentioned about having paid 50% of due wages from his own pocket in order to sustain the confidence and interest of wage seekers in the programme and to attract more wage seekers for participation in work with assurance of timely payment of wage.

In Mahur Block, people belonging to disadvantaged sections migrated to Adilabad District (Andhra Pradesh) as contract/bonded labourers for work in brick kilns, timber mills and construction works. The contractor paid ₹1,000–2,000 in advance. Along with ₹200–250 as daily wages, free board and lodging to such migrant labourers was provided. This could not be verified. In the same block, which has a total of 62 GPs, NGOs were implementing MGNREGS works in 28 GPs. They were being paid 2% of the total project expenditure as an honorarium amount. In GPs where NGOs were executing the works, measurements were recorded in the measurement book and submitted for verification (by JE).

As part of the district's water conservation drive, apart from works under MGNREGA was the construction of the *Vanrai Bandhara*s. These are temporary check dams constructed using empty cement bags. They are constructed in post-monsoon period to impound the running water in streams and rivulets. The construction is easy and done in groups. A total of 14,414 were constructed through community participation during 2010–11.

The focus on water conservation has also contributed to well recharging. The details provided by the district were: wells recharged—10,010; additional area irrigated—17,276 hectares (*rabi*).

The economic outcomes from the above details included: safety net for rural poor—30.65 lakh person-days; improved earning per family per year in the range of ₹15,000 to 20,000 per year.

During 2010–11, 10,000 dug wells at a cost of ₹7,500 per well was taken up while in the following year, 15,000 wells were dug (at a cost of ₹10,500 per well). Their material cost component was around 70%. The cost incurred per community dug well was ₹1.26 lakh during 2009–10, which increased to ₹1.90 lakh in the next financial year due to escalation in wages and material component. However, the cost incurred per dug well appears to be on a higher side as the ground water table of the district is at 120 feet.

In Pasaad village (Nanded Block), where the village community was collectively working on *Vanrai bori bundha*, the women's group informed that most of them did not have job cards and that it was very difficult to get employment during the lean season. In Shekapur GP, a *gangmate*—actually a labour contractor—was noticed.

Affirmative action to enhance the participation of marginalized community

Overall, 74% of small and marginal farmers, including 5.5% SCs and 7.5% STs, benefitted under well-recharging scheme.

As per information provided by the district, the water table had risen by 20 feet after recharging the open/dug wells. Near about 15,000 acres and 30,000 acres were brought under assured irrigation during 2010–11 and 2011–12, respectively. The recharge wells had brought about a smile on the faces of innumerable farmers whom it had benefitted in their agriculture-related work. About 17,276 hectares benefitted during the *rabi* season of 2011–12 and its (*rabi* crop) productivity increased by two-folds.

As a result, the district was able to save a lot of expenditure on requisitioning of water tankers as the root cause of the water scarcity was effectively addressed and ameliorated. The expenditure incurred on supplying drinking water tankers was brought to naught.

During the field visits, it was observed that physically handicapped persons and SC and ST families were given priority in the allocation of wells which was reminiscent of the efforts seen in Madhya Pradesh under the Kapildhara scheme.

Gajanna Vittal Rao of Dhamdari GP was provided with the recharge of his dried-up dug well. While he was earlier cultivating only two acres of his land, due to irrigation facility which became available now, he was able to cultivate 4.5 acres of his land. Similarly, Dondiram Krishan Kadam, belonging to ST community and also physically handicapped, got benefitted from the dug well scheme. Due to irrigation facilities, he shifted from cotton–soyabean cropping to sugarcane cropping. He harvested 40 tonnes per acre (minimum support price being ₹1,500 per tonne).

Grievance redressal mechanism

The grievance redressal mechanism was observed to be very weak in the district. Neither was a complaint register maintained nor was any complaint registered during the past five years. While social audits were organized, no shortcomings were observed. Also, their report was not available at the GP level. The awareness levels among the wage seekers regarding the toll-free number were very low.

Good practices

The district took up water harvesting and water conservation works as the major developmental programme for raising the ground water level through recharging existing wells, creation of soil and moisture conservation structures and arresting run-off water through the *Vanrai bori bundha* system. These soil and moisture conservation works executed in the last two to three years had led to improvement in the ground water table and availability of water in the district, as the district received normal rainfall during 2010–11.

The small and marginal farmers' purchasing power had considerably improved due to change in cropping system (a shift from rain-fed crops to irrigated crops, and also from subsistence farming to commercial farming) mainly due to assured life-saving irrigation facilities.

The district administration has leveraged MGNREGS for mitigating water scarcity in the district, with a passion that was clearly driven by the DPC who seems committed to transforming

MGNREGS from a relief work programme to an opportunity for creating sustainable assets for community development.

Notwithstanding the procedural weaknesses in the implementation of the programme, the district administration has worked with single mindedness to leverage MGNREGS to promote water conservation. Besides water conservation, the district has also encouraged the development of nurseries to promote plantation of horticulture crops such as *ber*, custard apple, *sapota*, citrus, *aanvla*, *kashid* and teak.

3.12 REPORT OF NATIONAL COMMITTEE FOR MGNREGS ADMINISTRATIVE AWARDS 2010–11: NARMADA DISTRICT (GUJARAT)[12]

Visit to Tilakwada

While there is convergence with the forest department as money is given to them, they spend money/execute the programme without following any of the provisions of the Act. No oversight by the 'Development' departments of the district or supervision by the District Collector was observed in this matter. Even social audit is not applicable to them. So on 'convergence' what we see is the opposite of what we wish to achieve through convergence. Of course, there is some resource mobilization as the forest department has other sources of generating revenue. Almost half the district is controlled by the forest department and hence working with them is needed in MGNREGS but this cannot be the approach. Instead of intervening and strengthening the tribes to negotiate with those with whom they have problems on a daily basis, MGNREGS serves as sops to keep the tribes happy and whether even this was achieved could not be verified during such a short period of visit.

While this is so in the forest areas, in the plain areas the biggest activity is road building and protection walls. While the area has many ravines, which does call for some degree of land levelling, but one does not understand the logic of taking up construction of protection walls as that are meant for contracting flowing water. This does not take place in the area. In the visiting team's opinion it is crucial that the district focuses on improving livelihoods through asset creation and works on

---

[12] This brief report has comments of K.S. Gopal who visited the district. Please see the summary and theme-wise reports for comments of K.B. Saxena.

individual lands. Here they claim community or joint-owned well as a unique feature.

All wells inspected had the beneficiaries incurring considerable expenditure on their own. They have also paid for the diesel set on their own. Beneficiary identification is done mostly by the village *Talatri*, a powerful revenue official. Hence, one cannot see the construction of wells as serving the most needy by providing an asset to a wider coverage of farmers with lower entitlements. The visiting team would not consider this manner of resource utilization for a small section of the community as serving the agenda of creating, improving and strengthening of assets for the poor households in the MGNREGS.

Despite the above, one does get a sense that the Gujarat Government is now waking up to MGNREGS as seen from recruitment of personnel for the programme and salaries paid to them. They are recruiting the staff now and these people are paid much better in comparison to their counterparts in other States. Thus, it is possible for Gujarat to catch up. But it is important that if Gujarat wants to do better and help its wage employment needy people, then it must improve and overhaul its systems. The gap in motivation between the permanent and senior government officials and the new recruits working at the implementation edge must be appropriately bridged. Convergence needs better understanding. Stress should be on pulling in place better systems rather than outsourcing difficult areas to other agencies. The attitude of senior officers needs to be changed from avoiding to face difficult problems to facing them up front, solving them and improving performance.

There is a lot to be done, for instance, on improving muster roll, the visiting team saw *kuccha* muster rolls as the e-muster rolls were not available. When the team saw these rolls in the office, it became clear that the workers whose names were not listed on the rolls when were not allowed to work 'works' were taken up.

To improve their performance, Gujarat must revisit both their ideas and systems and focus on enforcing the intent of the Act rather than implementing the scheme to suit the views of individual officials. One does not understand how an infrastructure-wise advanced State has three months' delay in wage payment. This is the most important problem to be tackled to show the pathway for improving MGNREGS performance in the State and especially this district which has a large number of tribal population and wherein except that land structure is ravine type, all other parameters are similar to what we see in the plain areas.

3.13 REPORT OF NATIONAL COMMITTEE FOR MGNREGS ADMINISTRATIVE AWARDS 2010–11: NICOBAR DISTRICT (ANDAMAN AND NICOBAR ISLANDS)[13]

District profile

Nicobar District covers an area of 1,841 sq. km and is located in the Bay of Bengal. The district was created on 1 August 1974 and comprises 22 islands, of which only 12 are inhabited. The district has a population of 42,068 persons as per the 2001 census and comprises three subdivisions, namely, Car Nicobar, Nancowry and Great Nicobar. The population density of Nicobar is 23 persons per square kilometre. The district is separated from the Andaman group of islands by a 10° channel. Car Nicobar Island, about 278 km south of Port Blair, is the district headquarters.

The district is predominantly inhabited by tribals. The tribal population has a traditional system of administration called Tribal Council (with the exception of three GPs consisting of seven villages, in Great Nicobar subdivision) in the district.

Observations

The district consists of smaller groups of Islands which are separated from each other and have poor connectivity. Keeping this in mind, three block-level teams have been constituted for implementation of MGNREGA. The programme is being implemented in all islands of the district in an effective manner.

The district was struck by the tsunami/earthquake in 2004 devastating almost the entire island. Relief and rehabilitation efforts—a massive logistic exercise, considering the remoteness and scatteredness of the islands—brought the life of Nicobarese, back to normalcy.

Car Nicobar is inhabited by the aboriginal tribal population and coconut plantation is their lifeline. Out of the total geographical area of 12,700 hectares, 9,027 hectares is covered with coconut plantation. In fact, the entire economic activity of Car Nicobar revolves round coconut plantation. However, due to large-scale damage and destruction of coconut trees during the tsunami and due to non-tending of plantations for a considerable period of time, productivity of the trees had decreased substantially.

Recognizing the importance of coconut in their lives and its traditional influence on economic and

[13] This brief visit report has comments of K.B. Saxena, Pradip Prabhu and Nilay Ranjan who visited the district.

social development, the Andaman and Nicobar Union Territory administration launched Car Nicobar Coconut Mission in the end of January 2009. The goal of the mission is to improve the quality of life of the people solely dependent on coconut for their livelihood by inducting new technologies into coconut-based farming and making coconut palm into 'Tree of Life' for Nicobarese.

Majority of plantation of coconut in the Island was unsustainable at the time of launch of the mission. Most of the plantations were senile and without any management. The low level of productivity was due to non-removal of senile palms, dense plantation with inadequate spacing and lack of proper management. There used to be no crown clearance, basin making and mulching operation.

Under the Mission, 15 demonstration plots of 20 hectares each in all the villages were created, using full package of technologies. It was envisaged that the demonstration plots would help the tribals in adopting this method of scientific cultivation in their own fields and that would transform their unsustainable plantation into a sustainable one.

The district administration informed that 14 plots had been fully completed and the remainder one was nearing completion. This could be achieved only because the district team had dovetailed the labour component (for creating the demo plot) with MGNREGA. Nicobarese take ownership of the work in the demonstration plot. The manual activities taken up for creation of demonstration plots included basin making, mulching, crown clearing, catch pit making and application of green manure and intercropping.

By dovetailing Coconut Mission with MGNREGS, the district team has generated 68,712 man-days of work, till date. While by generating wage employment the mission fulfilled the first objective of MGNREGS, by simultaneously creating sustainable plantation as durable assets of tribals, it fulfilled the secondary objective as well.

Now, tribals are gradually adopting the scientific method of cultivation in their own fields. The productivity of coconut has grown from 19 per palm to 40 per palm. Certainly, it has contributed in the upliftment of economic status of the Nicobarese.

The innovative initiative of the District Collector to introduce scientific management of (naturally overcrowded) coconut groves by reducing crown crowding for better access to sunlight, trimming tree growth and removal of senile trees, all leading to better yield, is an appreciable effort.

The initiative of converging the Coconut Mission scheme (which provided organic fertilizers and micro-nutrients and introduced scientific tree management inputs to the people), *Rashtriya Krishi Vikas Yojana* scheme (which introduced compositing to generate green manure as a very large extent of the top soil was washed away by the tsunami) and the MGNREGS scheme deserves recognition for both innovation and convergence.

The perspective of the District Collector to introduce productive community work, thereby also assisting in renewal of the community shattered by the extensive damage and loss of near and dear ones by the tsunami, deserves commendation in the light of the observation of the Chief Captain of the island Mr. Aberdeen Blair who said that NREGA was very beneficial to unemployed youth of the island as the joint family system (*tuhet*) was not able to offer them any cash income. He said that the programme of cultivating coconut as a commercial crop was new to the people. Coconuts as far as the people can remember were growing naturally. They collected coconuts and sold them to earn some cash income as there was no other source of cash. The other captains were, however, generally indifferent to the programme.

However, a few reflections on response of the administration to ravages of the tsunami and to the lifestyles of the tribal inhabitants of the island are necessary. The traditional villages in which *tuhet* houses were constructed in a compact area have been dismembered and now the houses have been dispersed alongside the roads. One would anticipate that fragmentation of once organically close joint families and their dispersal would result in the rapid erosion of a well-knit and gentle culture.

The introduction of 'scientific commercial coconut farming' into a community of traditional food gatherers and rotational cultivators would adversely affect the environmental lifestyles of these communities as also the knowledge and cultural traditions of ecological living imbibing deep respect to the requirements of Mother Nature.

The introduction of 'commercial perspectives' into a community hitherto following subsistence life styles in consonance with the environment and the needs of nature could upset the ecological fragility of the coral islands in the not-so-distant future.

The introduction of 'wage labour' and payment of wages in cash to individual beneficiaries in a societal structure of caring and sharing of extended families would definitely put these organically evolved eco- and human-sensitive community systems and cultures at grave risk of elimination.

The observations are being made notwithstanding the merit of the work, so that the gains of the present do not endanger the fruits of the past and sustainable futures of these ecological communities.

The Nicobarese are not oriented towards commercial cultivation of coconuts. The existing economy based on food gathering and rotational cultivation assures their subsistence and eco-friendly life style. This is why no urge in the community to take to scientific cultivation was in evidence outside the area of commercial plots. This is equally true of vegetable and fruit cultivation. They are participating in the project because local administration invests a lot of effort and resources in it. While the cash received for labour in the project is welcome, it does not appear likely that they would continue to put in this labour after the project funding is stopped. Besides, they feel unease at any innovation which has the potential of destabilizing their existing social organization and community control over productive resources.

Apart from the traditional ecological living, assured subsistence and relatively undifferentiated social organization, the perceived merits of which fail to attract them to commercial farming or surplus generation, the absence of a ready market for absorbing excess produce has also contributed to this lack of urge to adopt scientific cultivation. Though coconut produce is procured by the Andaman and Nicobar administration for marketing, it does not offer them an attractive price due to rejection of a sizable output on the ground of poor quality. Consumption markets are far away. Transport costs are high. There is no local market either for coconut or for excess vegetable and fruit produces. A tiny population of officials in Nicobar town meets its needs of vegetables and fruits either from backyard farming or from ships which pass through the island. Given the restrictions on the entry of outsiders into the area, this situation is not likely to change. Their level of contentment with existing living is quite high and there is no noticeable high demand for consumer products coming from outside. A local market for their surplus produce and demand for goods not produced by them could have triggered over a period, a pressing need for cash and therefore the urge to improve production to generate it.

The youth is certainly interested in a sustainable source of cash income to satisfy their changing needs having been better exposed to the life style of the outsider. MGNREGS offers it in a limited way. But sustainable income-generating programmes consistent with local ecology and culture would have to be taken up for this purpose. The youth are more likely to be drawn to non-farm employment if available than to take up farming. Even if they continue to participate in the project activities for earning cash, it seems doubtful if they have the necessary clout in the decision making in the *tuhet* to change the mode of production for this reason.

There is potential for taking up other works under MGNREGS which have not been explored. One such work is the scheme for restoration of tsunami-ravaged lands and fresh water bodies affected by salinity ingress. Labour input in such schemes can come from MGNREGS and material component to treat the soil can come from existing schemes of the Ministry of Agriculture and partly also from MGNREGS. The Deputy Commissioner needs assistance of experts for preparing such projects. This project would have the benefit of environmental restoration as well as of building productive assets.

The administration should progressively reduce labour input support in the coconut orchard scheme while continuing with extension, input and technology support. This would indicate whether the households constituting *tuhet*s are prepared to put in their unpaid labour for improving coconut cultivation initiated by the project on a sustainable basis.

The local administration should carefully watch the impact of the project on the social structure and its value system so that appropriate corrective interventions can be undertaken if destabilizing trends are noticed.

Since coconut produce is procured for marketing by the government agency, it should improve the level of returns from the produce which may perhaps incentivize local people to raise production and its quality with technological and input support from the local administration.

3.14 REPORT OF NATIONAL COMMITTEE FOR MGNREGS ADMINISTRATIVE AWARDS 2010–11: NIZAMABAD DISTRICT (ANDHRA PRADESH)[14]

District profile

Nizamabad District is located in the north-western region of the State. It is the second least populous and most backward district of Telangana region of Andhra Pradesh. According to the 2011 census, the district population is around 25.52 lakh, out of which 15% are SCs and 7% are STs. About 62.25%

[14] This brief visit report has comments of V. Suresh Babu and B. Panda who visited the district. Please see the summary and theme-wise reports for comments of K.B. Saxena.

of the population is literate. It is also reported that 17.6% of girls wed before the legal age of 18 years. The geographical area of the district is around 7,956 sq. km. About 22% of the total geographical area is under forest. The annual rainfall of the district is 1,036 mm. The climate of the district is characterized by a hot summer and generally dry weather, except during the south–west monsoon season. Nizamabad is predominantly an agricultural area. Frequently, agriculture is affected by drought. Hence, migration to the nearby towns and cities is severe. Paddy and sugarcane are the major crops in irrigated areas, while in dry regions, maize, jowar, bajra, cotton, soyabean, safflower, sunflower and pulses are cultivated. The demand for MGNREGS is high in the area where perennial crops are being cultivated such as sugarcane and turmeric. The total number of main workers are 9.7 lakh forming 41% of the total population against the State average of 38%. Cultivators (3.05 lakh) form 31.4% and agricultural labourers (2.27 lakh) form 23.4% of the main workers as per the 2001 census. There are 36 *mandal*s in the district.

Performance of MGNREGS in the district

The district has issued 4.01 lakh job cards covering 22.5% SCs and 11% STs. In total, 179.33 lakh person-days under MGNREGS have been generated in the district, from which, 23% of SCs, 14% of STs and 59% of women got benefitted. On an average, 45 days of employment is provided for registered SC households, 57 days for registered ST households and overall, 45 days of employment is generated per registered household. Out of 1.42 lakh approved works, only 1,092 works have been completed while another 23,435 works are in progress. About 75,989 households have completed 100 days of employment from which 20% of SCs and 13% of STs have benefitted. According to the MIS data dated 24 January 2012, 94 land development works and 12 Category IV works have been completed. Hundred per cent of wages are disbursed through post office. This indicates that the data for 2010–11 in the MIS has not been updated. There is huge unmet demand for work in the district.

Some of the registers maintained at the GP level relate to: job cards, works taken up, shelf of projects, land development projects, registers provided to SSS, work demand register, group demand slips and adult literacy among MGNREGS. Registers not maintained are complaint register, asset register and muster roll register.

Worksite facilities such as shade and crèche facilities are not provided. The Mandal Programme Development Officer (MPDO) informed that the

tarpaulin tents would be provided to each SSS before the onset of summer season.

In Khammarpalli *mandal*, Innayatnagar, land *patta* has been issued to forest dwellers under FRA with the authorized signatures of the District Collector, District Forest Officer and revenue department officials. However, the land is still under occupation of the forest department. Forest department officials do not allow the landholders to dig open well or bore well in their lands. However, they encourage the farmers to plant teak seedlings. In the land development estimate, bush clearance is also one of the components but fund allocated for the scheme is uniform without considering the quantum of bush/scrub jungle in a given plot. This leads to incomplete schemes due to underestimation of work/labour required. For example, usually if a tree is cut, the volume of work done is calculated based on the area covered by the shade of the tree. In practice, the canopy is considered without considering the girth at breast height, height of the tree and volume of wood cut (in cft). There is no evidence of the volume of work involved and accomplished with any photographs (pre, mid and post pictures) for the bush clearance activity.

It is also learnt from the wage seekers that the Village Development Committee decides the season or months to execute the MGNREGS works (basically to avoid labour shortage during cropping season). This practice denies the choice to the wage seeker whether to work in agriculture or MGNREGS or migrate. Another striking feature is incomplete projects. In Chittapur GP of Balkonda *mandal*, there are 164 approved projects with a budget of ₹48.18 lakh. However, the GP has completed only six works (3.6% of the total shelf of projects) and spent ₹10.71 lakh (22.3% of funds). This indicates that there is excess expenditure of funds on completed projects than the allocated amount. The MPDO informed that they did not get enough wage seekers to execute the MGNREGS works due to Sriram Sagar Project, three canals (viz., Kakathiya, Lakshmi and Drought canal) and four lift irrigation projects. About 150–200 power harvesters are operating in Chittapur GP of Balkonda *mandal* and Subriyal GP of Armoor *mandal*, due to shortage of labour as also to reduce cost of operations. It is high time to identify GPs of high work demand for executing MGNREGS for increasing fund use efficiency.

The land development works are technically flawed and badly designed besides lacking in proper planning. In Gongopalla GP, in one and half an acre of land, trenches are dug around the farm land in order to demarcate the land and to take up teak plantation in the next financial year. The farm has lost 3 m area all along the boundary of the farm land (1.5 m width of bund area and 1.5 m width of trench area) from cultivation. A simple measure like cultivating the land across the slope, that is, contour farming and rainwater harvesting in the ridge and furrows would have served the purpose. Due to scarcity of land for execution of MGN-REGS works, the Assistant Programme Officers (APOs) are taking up MGNREGS works in farm land which do not require any land development.

In Abbapur (M), Navipet *mandal*, Mekkala Praveen, 19 years old bearing job card no. 182360223030010144, was a student of Intermediate (plus 1) who got hurt while working under MGNREGS. Crowbar pierced into his foot and three fingers were completely damaged. He was admitted to the hospital and the fingers were replaced with steel rods. His hospital expenses have been borne from MGNREGS. Total expenses of ₹22,000 were reimbursed from the scheme. However, the teenager is presently not able to attend to his family farm operations or undertake any hard labour-oriented job. He has become permanently disabled and a burden to his family. Provision should have been made in the scheme to provide alternative livelihood to such cases. Further, the hospital charges should have been directly paid to the hospital rather than as reimbursement.

Affirmative action to enhance the participation of marginalized community

Land development programme is the major concern of the State Government for the year 2011–12. Hence, the district administration has given priority to the works on private lands. The permissible Category IV works can be implemented on lands on priority basis in an order (SC/ST/BPL/Land reforms/small and marginal farmers in that order). However, it is noticed that majority of the beneficiaries under this category belong to the OBC and APL families. In Nizamabad, it is found that most of the SC and ST land have rock sheet constraint. Under land development, if provision is made to clear the rock sheet, it will be of great benefit to individual farmer by increasing area under cultivation.

According to the APO, Velpur *mandal*, most of the farm land are covered with irrigated facilities. It is, therefore, difficult to identify the worksite for MGN-REGS. There is shortage of labour for MGNREGS.

Grievance redressal mechanism

The grievance redressal cell is headed by the Additional Project Director. Complaint register is not maintained at the GP level. Social audit is considered as the source of complaints. Action taken report on audits needs to be submitted to the social audit co-ordinator which in turn needs to be submitted to the State social audit cell. While social audits are conducted effectively, the public participation is not effective. It was brought to our notice that due to Telangana agitation, 1,800 pension holders were considered dead. The district administration had considered them dead and their pension accounts had been closed. Later, due to the intervention of the MPDO, pensions were restarted.

Based on the social audit report, the following punishments were imposed:

- POs/MPDOs: 4 (Enquiry ordered on four, Criminal cases filed in one case)
- APOs: 3 (Action initiated)
- TAs: 19 (Criminal cases filed in three cases)
- Field assistants: 108 (Criminal cases filed in three cases and rest are terminated)
- Mates: 198 (All terminated)

Good practices

Online attendance and measurement are carried out using Point of Sale (POS) machine and wages are disbursed through Point of Transaction Device (POTD). While taking attendance, thumb impression is taken to recognize the wage seeker. In case thumb impression is not recognized, photograph is taken using webcam. Once the snap is taken, the wage seeker is recognized in the group along with the implement which he/she has brought to the worksite and attendance is given. Measurements are recorded in the presence of the mate and two wage seekers of the concerned SSS group. Disadvantage of online attendance is that half-day attendance cannot be marked.

Biometric wage disbursement through the post office has been implemented on a pilot basis in this district. On an average, ₹105 is paid per person per day. Wages are paid maximum in a period of 15 days to one month from the date of closure of muster roll. There is technical convergence with Mandal Computer Centre, postal department, TATA Consultancy Services and Andhra Pradesh online. About 2% of the total expenditure is paid to the AP online. Of which 0.5% is paid to the branch post office (BPO) (the Community Service Provider) who disburses the amount to the wage seekers. The BPO is not paid any commission for the first 20 payments. For more than 20 payments, the BPO is paid 1.5% of the total transaction by MGNREGS. In total, the BPO is paid 2% of commission of the total wages disbursed.

Other observations

Record keeping

In all the *mandal*s, record keeping is excellent. The following registers are maintained in every *mandal* (Yelleredy, Nizamsagar, Nagareddypet, Lingampet, Tadwai, Varni Ditchpally and Jakarvpally) which was visited:

1. Muster roll watch register
2. Grievance register
3. Internal audit register
4. Fund transfer order (FTO) register
5. Review meeting register
6. Movement register
7. Block *panchayat* member (BPM) meeting register
8. Error register
9. Muster status register
10. Stock register
11. Wage FTO register
12. *Palli Sabha* register (GP level)

In Yelleredy, Nizamsagar, Nagareddypet, Varni and Ditchpally *mandal*s, the visiting team visited all the MPDOs' offices and verified all the records. The details of some workers from the Muster Roll Register were collected and tallied with the job cards of the workers working in the field. Payment has been made but none of the job cards was updated. The payment made electronically to the workers in the MPDO office computer was tracked and satisfied. However, in most cases, the payment was made within 14 days but not seven days as claimed by the DPC in his presentation. The delay was at the level of the BPO mostly. Because of the drought last year, a good number of workers worked in MGNREGS without migrating to Hyderabad.

Some MSc students were working in MGNREGS. Also it was found that the field assistant was using the pass machine for e-biometric attendance. Every field assistant, TA and EC has machine for attendance, measurement and check measurement, respectively. Job cards have not been updated for years. Exclusion is minimal.

In Lingampet mandal, Perumalla GP, the asset register was not found. The field assistant G. Laxman has not updated the job cards. Exclusion was observed.

In Chithyal GP in Tadwai *mandal*, exclusion is very much visible as the SC colony residents have been denied work recently because of the field assistant and the landlord lobby coming together.

In Jakarpally mandal, record keeping is poor. There is glaring exclusion as a number of SC women and men have not been given work although they have been demanding work. The field assistant has denied them work. The PO of the *mandal* has not taken any initiative to solve this problem. Mrs Velju Auranna has been demanding work for the last seven months, she has been denied of work by the field assistant. The PO has not taken any action on the social audit reports.

Positive recognition/achievements

The following achievements are observed:

1. Social audit has been done regularly.
2. Demand process is perfect in some GPs.
3. Reasonable degree of capacity building has been done in terms of training of the field assistant, mate, APO and MPDO.
4. Transparency level in the process in many GPs is good. All works undertaken, job card holders who worked and the number of days they worked were mentioned on the walls of visible places in large letters for public display.
5. Distress migration has been considerably reduced.
6. Payment is made within 14 days although in many cases payment has been made within eight days.
7. E-biometric machine is used for attendance; measurement is very good. This was personally checked and found its working sound.

Deficiencies

The following deficiencies are noticed:

(i) Job cards have not been updated in most of the villages.
(ii) Role of the GP is passive.
(iii) Deliberate exclusion of SC households is visible.
(iv) Monitoring in some *mandal*s is poor.

3.15 REPORT OF NATIONAL COMMITTEE FOR MGNREGS ADMINISTRATIVE AWARDS 2010–11: PITHORAGARH DISTRICT (UTTARAKHAND)[15]

District profile

Pithoragarh district is the eastern most district of Uttaranchal, sharing international boundary with two countries: China and Nepal. The district is divided into four subdivisions (Pithoragarh, Didihat, Dharchula and Munsyari) and eight blocks (Berinag,

---

[15] This visit report has comments of V. Suresh Babu, K.B. Saxena (with writing inputs of Rajesh Mall) and Ashwini Kumar who visited the district.

Dharchula, Didihat, Gangolihat, Kanalichina, Munakot, Munsyari and Pithoragarh).

One of the special features of administration in this hill district is that the *patwari* has been conferred with police powers as well. According to the Central Statistical Organisation, the district has an area of 7,110 sq. km with total population of 4.62 lakh residing in 1,632 revenue villages organized into 669 GSs.

A significant percentage of the population belongs to tribal and weaker sections. Majority of them are Hindus, followed by Buddhists. The literacy rate of the district is 76.48%. The elevation of the district ranges from 500 m above sea level in the valleys in the south to over 700 m in the snow-bound Himalayas in the north and north-west. The climate is related to altitude and elevation. January is the coldest month with a mean maximum temperature of 10°C at heights of 2,000 m above sea level. The annual rainfall in the district is 36.7 cm. A large part of the district lies under perpetual snow and a considerable area is rocky and barren. Cultivation is, therefore, limited to the river valleys and the gently sloping hills. The usual limit of cultivation is up to 2,000 m above sea level. Arable land is small and land holdings are small and fragmented. There are large unused wastelands as well. Women workforce is very dominant in the district.

Performance of MGNREGS in the district and some observations from the field

Pithoragarh is a Phase 3 district. Out of the registered 0.827 lakh households in the district, 0.822 lakh have been issued job cards of which 22% belong to SCs while 4% to STs.

However, only 59% of job card holders were provided with employment. About 21.46 lakh persondays were generated out of which 24.5% SC, 3% ST, 71% Other category and 36% women benefitted.

Households completing 100 days were very meagre (0.17%). Keeping in mind the limited availability of livelihood options and terrain of the district, the demand for MGNREGS employment is high. However, the reach of MGNREGS to workers/job card holders is very limited, according to figures provided on the website.

Pithoragarh District was nominated for its 'Innovative Project of Fodder Development'. Fodder development programme was initiated by the DPC. The Committee held interactions with the GP Secretaries and *Pradhans*, block and *Zila Panchayat* elected representatives including BDOs.

During the interaction, Smt Sunitha Waliya, President, Din GP, informed that Napier grass had been cultivated for the last two years. In both the years, it was sown/planted in the month of June and harvested during August.

Hence, green fodder was available only for a period of three months. Out of 200 households in her village, only 50 households benefitted under this fodder development programme. The fodder raised through cultivation is insufficient as every household has around 6–10 grazing animals. Every household is allowed to harvest 50 kg (*doka*) of green fodder per day. Jeevan Singh, *sarpanch* of Darsu (Munsyari Block), informed that fodder cultivation was being carried out in 20 hectares of land and 90 families were beneficiaries of this programme.

A women's SHG was managing the distribution of fodder. However, availability of fodder during the winter season was very scarce. The quantity of green fodder feed required for cattle depends on the quality of breed and genetic type. The milk yield per cattle varies from 200 ml to 500 ml per time depending on the breed.

As part of the fodder development programme, two-hectare plot of revenue land is being fenced by piling of stones to a height of 1–2 m to prevent entry of stray animals. The total expenditure per two hectares is ₹3.41 lakh per year of which ₹2.45 lakh is towards labour component and ₹0.96 lakh as material component (including land development, fencing, trenching, vermi-composting pits, etc.). For each plot, two vermiculture units (3 m × 2.5 m × 2 ft) are being maintained. The horticulture department is providing the technical know-how along with the earthworms. Usually, 80 kg *MP chari* seeds and two quintal of Napier grass slips are procured from Vivekanada labs, an ICAR unit at Almora. About 80 kg of *jai* seed is also sown in rotation. An additional 10% of seed material is procured for gap filling.

In Baravey GP, about 348 households (out of 350) have been issued job cards. About 70 of these households are SC wage seekers. It was informed by the village community that maintenance of potato crop is difficult due to monkey and wild boar menace. Hence, fencing of their plot is of prior importance. In the village there are 523 cows, 149 buffaloes and 1,349 goats. In this GP, migration is rare. Apart from the fodder development programme, tea development programme is also being implemented under MGNREGS land development category. Better yield genotypes are provided by the horticulture department to improve productivity. GP inventory with information on every household is generated and maintained by the GP officials. The inventory indicates the families which do not possess cultivable land and those without cattle.

In Kimkhola GP (Dharchula Block), there are 83 households including 11 SC and 34 ST households. Most of them are dependent on farming. The members of ST families are virtually landless agricultural labours as most of their owned land (around 10 *nali* or 0.5 acre) is located on the rocky ridge areas and therefore uncultivable. Their main occupation is selling fuel wood and grass (collected from the forest). They have worked under MGNREGS for a period ranging from 45 to 60 days. About 20–25 households cultivate fodder in the civil soyam or *van panchayat* land lying barren or unused. They usually migrate to Giri to work as labourers on road construction sites.

Hence, despite heavy demand for MGNREGS employment by these wage seekers, very limited number of works was executed by the GP. During 2010–11, only four works—protection wall, water harvesting structure, repair and formation of irrigation canal and fodder development—were taken up. On an average, ₹8–10 lakh is the GP budget for MGNREGS. In fact, as it emerged from interactions, there is a huge demand for taking up canal work and construction of as many as four check dams in the GP.

It can hence be inferred that the implementing officials/agencies are not clear about the MGNREGS operation guidelines. Further, there is no effective monitoring by the block and district administration to rectify the deviations. None of the wage seekers' job cards has been updated. It was observed in the muster roll sheets that about 70–80% of the workforce were women in each of the work executed. On an average, only 45–60 days of employment was being provided by the GPs. Wage seekers were not aware about the issue of individual dated receipts, their rights and entitlements. *Capacity building and updating the skills of all the stakeholders are very essential.* Capacity building should not be considered as a one-time affair. The *sarpanch* was not aware of the FRA.

The cultivation of fodder species [oat (*jaee*), MP *chari*, Napier grass, etc.) on rotation on civil-soyam (which is government revenue) land in fenced plots, ranging from a minimum of two hectares to up to five hectares, has been initiated in the district since 2010–11 in all the eight blocks and 41 GPs. This experimentation is not unique in the district as Champavat District has already toyed with the scheme of fodder development with an active policy push from the State Government. Then, there is a history of Napier cultivation in the district since the 1980s as reported by local villagers and farmers. Therefore, the fodder development scheme has come out of earlier deliberation and experience in the region.

Wage seekers informed that their wage negotiation capacity had improved mainly due to MGNREGS. The minimum wage paid under MGNREGS is ₹120, while the market rate is ₹140. There is no wage discrepancy between men and women.

Wages were distributed within a period of two to three weeks. Under MGNREGS, single saving bank account is being operated per household. The wages are remitted to a single family account, irrespective of wages earned by wife or husband or their dependents. It was also noticed that every individual was paid full wages (₹120) without considering their work output. According to wage seekers, worksite facilities were not provided.

In 2009–10, the district had ₹37.05 crore but spent only ₹23.44 crore and made employment available to only 0.4667 lakh households in which SCs constituted about 33.75%, STs 5.46% and women (20.41%). About 32,786 households demanded work and 32,554 got employment. And only 446 households completed 100 days with Munsyari Block accounting for only 19 households. (This was a clear case of very low penetration of MGNREGA; it is a Phase III district and the work started only in 2008.) Under Category IV work, only 17 households were provided employment. Major category of work undertaken was water conservation. About 2,959 households were not given unemployment allowance. The issue of delay in payment is not addressed as there is no information about it in the MIS.

However, in the next financial year, the performance of MGNREGS has improved in the district. In 2011, the total money available to the district was ₹37.05 crore and the district spent ₹23.44 crore (the MIS data appears incorrect as the same information is reflected under the category of expenditure in 2009–10). About 81,662 households were issued job cards; 48,667 households demanded work and 48,336 households got the work. However, compared to 2009–10, 3,800 households completed 100 days of work. Under Category IV, only 17 households were beneficiaries. The average wage was ₹105.96 with wage rate of ₹120. The unemployment allowance was not paid to 528 households with Pithoragarh Block accounting for 485 such households. Delay in payment occurs; the usual gap is between 16 days and 30 days (only workers in 10 muster rolls were paid after 90 days).

A site in Munakot Block (the site was selected by the district administration) in Barabe Panchayat was inspected. The DPC showed it under the fodder development programme. Muster rolls were inspected; the culture of wage payment without any measurement is evident. The job card of Laxman

Chandra (with job card no. 35110080390022105) was also inspected. Job cards are not filled; the district administration cited the shortage of Employment Guarantee Assistant as the reason for this.

From the interaction of few wage seekers, it was not clear if the fodder work has been undertaken with their consent and participation as the GS meetings are not frequent and MGNREGS GS meetings do not take place as required.

Affirmative action to enhance the participation of marginalized community

During 2010–11, only 97 works were completed and another 7,047 works were in progress or suspended during the year. Out of the works completed, 37% related to flood control, 28% to Category III works (irrigation canals) and 16% related to renovation of traditional water harvesting bodies. *Only one work under irrigation facilities to SC/ST/IAY/LR beneficiaries was completed.*

Grievance redressal mechanism and deviations in implementation

No complaints were lodged at the GP and block levels. In fact, the complaint register was not maintained at village but at the GP level.

The district follows the practice of making the payment without the measurement book.

The violation of labour–material ration was noticed and two such cases are cited here after investigation.

The example is of muster roll number 3511001009/FP/346 in Munsyari Block (Table 3.5).

Table 3.5 Particulars of muster rolls issued, utilized and payment made without muster roll and measurement book in Pithoragarh during 2010–11

Blocks	Number of muster rolls issued	Number of filled-in muster roll	Wage disbursement without muster roll	Muster rolls without measurement book
Berinag	3,686	3,165	2,226	3,165
Dharchula	3,500	3,498	3,389	3,498
Didihat	2,150	1,618	1,191	1,618
Gangolihat	4,829	4,780	4,411	4,780
Kanalichina	3,602	3,562	2,386	3,562
Munakot	3,338	3,232	2,091	3,232
Munsyari	3,509	3,494	2,215	3,494
Pithoragarh	3,361	2,976	2,932	2,976
Total	27,975	26,325	20,841	26,325

As per the MIS data, the work was not included in the Annual Plan but it was started on 21 January 2010 (the sanction number is 26 and work sanction date is 21 January 2010); the total amount spent on material is ₹124,070, whereas on labour, zero expenditure has been shown! How can it be possible? Another work is 3511001076/FP/299 in Munsayari Block, where similar story has been repeated; on material the amount spent is ₹52,150, but on labour there is no entry (assuming zero expenditure). Interestingly, the work sanctioned date and the work started date are the same, i.e. 20 March 2010; this is too efficient for the hills.

Good practices

On the basis of the livestock census of 2007, the requirements of green and dry fodder for about 5.07 lakh livestock and equines were about 23.22 lakh and 10.32 lakh metric tonnes, respectively. Additionally, about 12.88 lakh metric tonnes of fodder (roughage) per annum was also required for the district. Therefore, 55.47% of fodder deficit is noticed in the district.

While almost every household has livestock, animal husbandry in hills is entirely in the hands of women. Women have to undergo severe hardships to fetch fodder. Old or young, graduate or illiterate, none of them is excluded from this drudgery. About 42 deaths were officially reported during 2010–11 and 280 animal deaths occurred due to foraging in the forest.

Then, poor quality and deficiency of fodder adversely affected the production of milk and other by-products. The District Magistrate being a veterinary doctor initiated the fodder development programme. This programme was projected as a women-centric scheme—of the women, by the women and for the women; it was initiated during September 2010 in the district. It is implemented under 'Land Development' category of the permissible work. The aim of the project is to eradicate 'Feminization of Poverty'. The total implementation cost was pegged at ₹17.15 crore.

The main objectives of this programme are to:

- reduce drudgery of women,
- reduce distance travelled by women every day to the forests,
- provide good quality fodder for animal at the GP itself and
- increase milk production.

The long-term objective of the programme is to ensure optimum utilization of scare land in hill areas.

Table 3.6 Phase-wise implementation of the fodder development programme

Phase period	Crop	No. of GPs	Total area (in hectare)	Total cost (in crore)
Phase I (September 2010–March 2011)	Oats (*jaee*)	42	142	2.24
Phase II (July 2010–December 2010)	Hybrid Napier and *MP chari*	122 (including 42 of Phase I)	394	6.78
Phase III (September 2010–March 2011)		162 (including 122 of Phases I and II)	520	813

The scheme is an innovative convergence of MGNREGS and the fodder development department with the active technical support of the following departments/agencies:

1. animal husbandry for technical expertise
2. RES for estimate preparation and technical sanction
3. rural development for implementation
4. DRDA for record keeping and fodder distribution by SHGs of the concerned GP and providing chaff cutter through SGSY infrastructure fund
5. NGOs for monitoring and impact assessment

The phase-wise implementation of the programme is given in Table 3.6.

Social benefit

Alternative fodder was now available for almost a month (four to five cuttings of *jaee* crop) in the lean season, reducing their drudgery—about half of their time is spent in trekking in the forest for fodder. Around 45% to 55% beneficiaries were women belonging to weaker sections (SC/ST).

Economic benefit

There is an increase in the number of person-days due to high proportion of labour component (70–75%). The programme ensured additional wages from MGNREGS (₹120) and money was earned from the sale of excess fodder.

Other benefits

The programme facilitated soil and moisture conservation. There was an increase in milk yield due to availability of quality fodder.

Overall impression and benchmark

Leadership and commitment was excellent. (The District Collector's role is quite significant as he had led the implementation from the front both as Chief Development Officer whose office was the nodal agency for the programme in 2009–10 and also as DPC/District Magistrate of the district.)

Innovation

Needs to be examined by the experts. It should be stopped due to adverse impact on environment and equity. Ecological sustainability of cultivating Napier grass, etc. is doubtful.

Social equity

Social equity looks poor. The DPC and his team need to be sensitized to equity issues.

Integrity of process and personnel

Integrity of process and personnel is found to be good, but procedural violations of the provisions and operational guidelines are routine; this needs to be curbed for the robust success of innovation.

Sustainable outcome

The outcome needs to be tracked over time (at least three years) and examined if it has potential to reduce the drudgery of women and also raise milk productivity and income of wage seekers. Caution needs to be taken that it does not lead to substitution of the entire MGNREGS by a single scheme of fodder development.

Accountability and transparency

Accountability and transparency looked satisfactory, but the district needs to act vigorously to implement the provisions of proactive disclosures. Social audit is notional and needs a thrust in the region.

Issues requiring attention

1. Violation of revenue law: diversion of use of government revenue land

Most of the fodder development pogramme plots are on civil-soyam land. Civil-soyam land definitionally comes under the forest area and is owned by the revenue department. However, the usufruct rights belong to the local people. The productivity of these lands is very low, and such land areas are generally used for grazing of animals. Importantly, this category of land can also be allotted for the construction of *panchayat ghar*, schools, hospitals, rehabilitation of people caused by natural calamities such as floods, earthquakes and landslides and different welfare-related programmes such as SC and ST settlements.[16] In some cases, the afforestation programme has been initiated on such land.

Hence, civil-soyam is the *only* type of land available to the government in its *land bank* for meeting multifarious needs, notably developmental activities/initiatives. Such land is not only in short supply but also the only reserve land available from which *patta*s to landless/shelterless poor are awarded. In the villages visited, there were several families that were landless (notably tribals and SCs) and several who were waiting for allotment of land *patta*s.

As this precious revenue land has competing and priority-based uses, unilaterally and uniformly diverting its use for cultivating fodder on a large scale is not within the powers of a District Collector. Legally, only the State Government has the power to divert its uses. Hence, it is a violation of the State revenue regulations. Also, diversion of revenue land for private benefit can lead to social conflict and unstability.

At the most, such land should be used only to develop a nursery for raising fodder species, which can be distributed free of cost to villagers in order to encourage them to grow it on private land.

2. Land intended for collective benefit being utilized for individual (groups) benefit

When an asset for distribution is created out of common land (fodder in this case), there has to be equal incentives and benefit for all. There is no equitable system of distributing the *chara*/fodder harvested. Ironically, it is based on the number of milch cattle holdings. It implies that people with a larger number of livestock get the lion's share of free harvest, while those not having cattle (or less cattle) are deprived of the rightful share.

Utilization of government land for collective benefit has to factor in needs, demands and priorities of different sections of society. Clearly, the choice of all groups in the village, notably the socially and economically marginalized, was not taken into account. As one villager said, '*Hamara jameen humse maanga, aur jaee laga diya*' (We were asked to give our land to the administration and *jaee* was cultivated in it). The choice of *chara* in a way serves the needs and aspirations of farmers/families with bigger land and livestock holdings. It is indeed diverting the benefits from common land to select people. It has become a State-sponsored *chara* scheme for the well-off people.

[16] G.S. Mehta, *Development of Uttarakhand: Issues and Perspectives* (New Delhi: APH Publishing, 2009).

3. Usurping of collective land by powerful/well-off social groups in the village

Under the programme, two- to five-hectare plots of civil-soyam land—by and large lying unutilized or fallow—belonging to the GS have been identified in 41 GPs. These have now been fenced with a 1.5 m stone wall. However, in one place, it was observed that the land selected was disputed as it jointly belonged to five brothers of an SC family, who had at one point of time been allotted *patta*s which were later withheld due to some government notification. They were cajoled in some way or the other by the GS/*Pradhan* to consent to offering this land for fodder cultivation. Hence, a land meant for their individual use and benefit is now being used for *chara vikas*. *The cultivation fodder on lands which are under dispute raised by any SC/ST family should be immediately stopped.*

Besides, the benefit of rightfully harvesting free fodder from common land is too strong a temptation (for well-off families) for cornering such a land. In the future, it will become difficult to divert the use of such land or restore it to its rightful owner.

Past experiences point out to the fact that there is a concerted effort by the powerful sections to ensure that no revenue land is given to landless persons from the SC/ST households on the pretext that it is required for school, temple, etc. in the future. Hence, the scheme inadvertently allows such people to corner precious revenue land for their benefit through the back door. This manner of utilization of government land for fodder cultivation will create both huge demand for its extension to other government lands by powerful interest groups which will be difficult to resist.

4. Ecological ramifications of large-scale cultivation of non-native fodder species

Three species, namely, Napier, *MP chari* and oat (*jaee*), have been selected for cultivating green fodder on the plots. A few things emerge which are noted here.

The species were chosen and cultivated unilaterally. No discussions in the GS/with locals took place to factor in their choice. However, there is acceptance of the fodder variety among locals and some studies indicate marginal increase in milk quantity of milch animals.

A vital missing link is that not even a single of traditional species of fodder, which have grown here over centuries, is suited to local ecology, and to which local breed of cattle is adjusted has been considered in even a single plantation. Locals pointed out how traditional species[17]—each having different nutritional content (say fat, lactose, etc.) and naturally regenerative—had disappeared over time in the forests and grazing lands. Locals pointed out to nearly 50 such traditional varieties of fodder grass which have disappeared.

There is hence the need for considering traditional species for cultivation both as a means of reviving traditional knowledge and species and long-term protection checking against monoculture and hybrid varieties which are non-native and not self-generating. Locals did express interest on growing traditional species. The possibility of getting their germ-plasm from the Indian Agricultural Research Institute (IARI) and experimenting plantation must be explored.

There is a history of Napier cultivation in the district since the 1980s, as pointed out by one of the progressive farmers, Mr Jeevan Negi, a Krishak Bharti Award recipient. However, since the seeds/stems are provided by the horticulture/agriculture department and there is a booklet of the IARI on the propagation of Napier cultivation in hill areas, the selection of species has government/institutional backing.

The long-term ecological ramifications of cultivating only these species on a mass scale in Pithoragarh, keeping in mind nutrition content, soil, climate, altitude and livestock factors, need to be examined. Napier, for instance, is native to Africa (Uganda) and can be grown in areas located at a sea level up to 2,000 m. However, in the hills (Pithoragarh is at an altitude of 1,852 m), there is no seed formation and stems/roots have to be used for regeneration (sourced from the IARI).

While Napier can be harvested for two to five years, its protein content is only 5–10% and it dries in the case of frost. It is not a soil binder and it requires stipulated amount of cow dung manure in the fields (implying cost) for maintaining the nitrogen content of the soil. The possibility of the plantations requiring fertilizer in few years' time cannot be ruled out. No test of soil pre- and post-cultivation has been done.

5. Equity and sustainability issues

There are inequities in the scheme. No norms/rules have been created or record keeping done on harvesting of the fodder, a much sought-after and precious

commodity, available free as a result of this cultivation. As a result, it will never be possible to know who is exploiting this resource at the village level.

The fodder is distributed on the basis of actual need of a household determined by the number of livestock (milch animals) a family owns. So, the well-off families with more cows and buffaloes have the natural right to harvest larger quantity of *chara*, while those who have lesser number of animals (say one/ couple) will reap a pittance. *And the poor/landless that have no cattle are hence out of the programme's benefits.*

Well-off families have hybrid/cross-breed variety of milch animals (such as Frizian and Jersey cows) which consume more fodder, thereby giving them a natural right to demand more fodder. So, not only are the big hybrid animals beneficiaries, it is also the genetic character of animals (hybrid animals are dependent on this type of fodder and not adjusted to locally available species) which is driving the force of what fodder to grow.

Also, while a poor family may work as wage labour in the project for developing the plot and its cultivation, a well-off family would obtain the fodder-harvest share despite minimal or no labour contribution. While labourers working on a plot are residents of different habitations scattered over a distance in the same village (typically a village has two to four habitations; *tog*), only residents of (one) *tog* where the plot is located primarily reap the harvest.

In no place is an SHG distributing the fodder. By and large, it is the *Pradhan*'s discretion. The harvest is made on a first-come first-served basis, with no predetermined norms for setting a time and date for harvest, known to all. The *Pradhan* announces the time of harvest, with a message being sent out in the villagers.

The free availability of fodder on the basis of livestock holding is also an inducement for the well-off to buy more animals, aggravating the inequity further. So, the well-off not only have more land available to them, but are also the beneficiaries of government subsidy through the *chara vikas* programme. It will lead to social reinforcement of the existing iniquitous power structure in the village. After all, the well-off in the village try to capture public resources through a variety of sources.

As the effort to cultivate *chara* and distribute it free of cost is government sponsored and based on subsidy, a big question arises on the sustainability of *Chara Vikas Yojana* once it is withdrawn from the ambit of NREGS. When the question of how the plantations will survive without government

[17] These include (local names, based on pronunciation): *vaaling, baanjh, chiuraa, guvraal, koiraal Auns, Betula* (creeper), *Kalpi ghaans* (grass), *Kaabhar, Kveyraal, Kailonch, kheduan, kharpoo, baanjh, falyaat, timulaa, khooniyaa* and *kataunch.*

supervision and subsidy was posed to the community in one of the GPs, they said that since the scheme had acceptance of villagers and was providing benefit to all, they would continue with cultivation through collective donations and effort.

A contribution (*anshdaan*) amount of ₹50 per month will be charged from each household which will be used to buy seeds and maintain the plot. The plot will remain open only for six months. A similar practice was resorted to for *Van panchayat* land. Maintaining the plantation would involve substantial costs in terms of seed procurement, irrigation (already in one of the sites it was observed that piped water being brought to the fields), engaging a watchman, manure, etc. Hence, an adverse fallout could be that the very poor who were not in a position to contribute would be out of it.

The issue of fodder development needs a separate treatment as it was not clear from the interactions with the villagers/wage seekers why the district administration shifted to cultivating Napier grass for fodder for the cattle without much consultation with local villagers/wage seekers. The ecological issue and the long-term sustainability of Napier cultivation also needs to be looked into. The issue of distribution of fodder among the wage seekers was not clear though the district administration refered to SHGs of women but on the site, the wage seekers were not aware of formation of SHGs. It is likely that the fodder development programme benefits relatively wealthy and dominant groups/individuals in the village. A cursory livestock analysis suggests that people belonging to the General category own more cattle than SC/ST and OBC; therefore, it is important for the district administration to consider equity aspects of the fodder development scheme. (*There was no evidence that the district administration has been willingly ignoring the equity; it comes out as one of unintended consequences of the design and implementation issue of the policy.*) From district administration's own evaluation of the fodder scheme it is clear that at this stage SHGs are rare and exception. *Gram Vikas Adhikari* Deepak Bhatt could not explain the process used by SHGs for fodder distribution. Though it appeared that the fodder development scheme has been top-down, it has brought MGNREGS to the grassroots. Also, fodder development has been undertaken in the civil-soyam land rather than on the *van panchayat* land which could have been much better for local villagers. Some policy corrections are required that cannot be suggested by this visiting team.

The member also visited a site in Nachni GP at Munsyari Block (Bhainskhal village) where the land development work had started for cultivating Napier grass/*Jaee* grass. It is found that job cards are not filled; photos are missing from job cards in Nachni (can also be verified from the MIS data on job cards). The wage seekers complained about trekking long distance for the work; since it is less than 5 km, they do not get extra wage for transport. The Ministry of Rural Development (MoRD) needs to relax the guidelines for transport allowance in hill areas. Bhainskhal village had only 89 job cards and only 57 households demanded work and 57 got the employment as per the MIS. The wage seekers on the site complained about lack of MGNREGS work in the village; many women also complained about injuries during work. The medical assistance needs to be provided as per the provisions of the Act. Interestingly, the district team especially BDO (PO) could not show muster rolls for the work. When asked, wage seekers reported that the work had been started almost 15 days ago. The BDO showed a document that suggested that the work had started on 15 November 2011 but he could not show the muster rolls for the work.

The practice of maintaining *kuccha* muster roll seems to be rampant in the district. Local progressive farmer and journalist Jeevan Singh confirmed the practice. The member discussed with Champa Devi w/o Anil Kumar and Malli Devi w/o Chandar Ram about the challenges of land development in the hilly terrain. They informed that the fodder development programme was liked by the wage seekers because of their need for green fodder. The job card of Kamla Devi regd. no. 0507-8373 was inspected whose house was in the vicinity of the worksite; it was not filled properly. The women of the village and at worksite, however, showed a lot of awareness about the entitlements/rights under MGNREGS.

On 28 November 2011, Durlekh village in Didihat Block was visited. The member was accompanied by Mr J.C. Pant (Extension Training Officer, officiating District Development Officer) and other officials. Smt Pushpa Devi, *Gram Pradhan*, Durlekh GP, was present on the fodder development site in the village; she informed that the decision of starting the fodder development work was taken by the GS. The project cost was estimated to be ₹493,600 in an area of three hectare of civil-soyam land. As per muster rolls, generally 20 wage seekers worked on the project. *Gram Vikas Adhikari* Shri Nandan Lal explained that the work was started in July 2011 (administrative sanction was given on 6 July 2011); muster rolls were inspected and job cards of wage seekers were also checked. The practice of maintaining *kuccha* muster rolls continues; however, the wages reported in the muster rolls were reflected in the postal account of the wage seekers. Wage seeker Shobhan Singh confirmed that he was paid ₹1,440 in his account no. 2222704. He also explained that the work was undertaken on the site. The job cards are not properly filled. Wage seekers Pushkar Singh with job card no. 85609 (he worked 14 days) and Dewan Singh with job card no. 13480 were satisfied with MGNREGS work and expressed no grievance. After inspecting the worksite, the team proceeded to Jorashi post office located in the market. Mr Mahiman Singh Vora, the branch post master, is also a cloth merchant and keeps his branch post office in excellent conditions.

6. Non-use of van panchayat *land for* Chara Vikas Yojana

An important missing element of the scheme is non-involvement of the age-old institution of *van panchayat* and non-use of its already existing considerable tracts of common village land. It would have been a good idea to engage its functionaries for discussion on growing fodder on their land with traditional species as their jurisdiction is related to similar issues such as collection of forest produce fodder and grazing. This would have empowered them to take up such a scheme through collective effort.

On an average, each *van panchayat* roughly has about 100–200 acres/hectares of land[18] meant for common usage (say grazing, collection of non-timber forest products, etc.) by its constituent villages. Traditionally GS members constitute the *van panchayat*. In most cases, such land is both lying unutilized and in a degraded/wasteland condition. This land is not in the control of the forest department and hence it does not take the initiative to develop it.

There is a need to regenerate this land through fencing, afforestation and plantation of species such as bamboo and traditional fodder grasses and turn it into productive and ecological assets. NREGS could provide the labour input for utilizing this land, which could lead to consolidation of existing collective decision making for development of land and strengthening of traditional knowledge base.

Van panchayat is an institution established as a result of a long struggle by villagers against appropriation of forest by the colonial government. Its land has clearly defined boundaries and the institution has an acceptance among the local people and therefore legitimacy jurisdiction. At the moment,

the forest department has not undertaken any work (except for afforestation and fencing in some areas).

Surprisingly, such a vital collective resource is lying unutilized.

7. Poor shelf of projects based under NREGS

The range of projects that can be undertaken under NREGS is poor. Other than the overarching *Chara Vikas Yojana*, other activities undertaken include construction of canals (*nahar*), check dams, check walls, compost pits and ponds (the later two only were adjacent to fodder plantations).

A glaring omission is near non-existence of Category IV (beneficiary-oriented) activities. At several places, the poor pointed out that there were an urgent need of small water storage structures, removal of stones, etc. to make their land cultivable and small watershed activities. There is also a need to develop individual land of the poor (mainly the SCs and STs) who have very small land holdings, thereby empowering them in the process.

Watershed (harvesting rainwater, snowmelt, etc.) and land development activities on private land will not only allow most efficient use of small agricultural land holdings but turn the unutilized land into productive assets.

8. Loopholes in the NREGS work

The most glaring shortcoming is of record keeping, mainly the maintenance of various registers and job cards of workers. It is in a poor shape with the potential to create tremendous amount of distortion. Muster rolls were missing and job cards were incomplete in terms of entries, filling up of details, absence of photographs, etc. Most of the recordings were on *kuccha* basis. No separate NREGS register has been made at the GS level and no discussions on it or shelf of projects has been recorded.

Job cards were, by and large, with the *Pradhan* and the beneficiaries were largely clueless about the number of days they had worked and wages earned. No medical kits were available (despite being purchased) on the worksite and no compensation was awarded in case of injuries. Workers had to compulsorily bring their own equipment (else they would not be eligible to seek work) and no purchase of equipment from allocated funds was paid as wage.

A flat rate of ₹120 per person per day was paid as wage rather than piece rate arrived on the basis of actual output of work. While women wage labourers were in equal number, none of them was made mate. Worksite facilities for them and otherwise were absent.

Despite demand, very few households were able to get 100 days of work. Only four cases of completions of 100 days were recorded. And they did not seem to

---

[18] There are some *panchayat*s which do not own such land.

be from the very poor or the really deserving worker. By and large, there was a huge demand–supply gap as the average availability of work was for 40–50 days annually. Rotation of work was being resorted to and by and large it was the discretion of the *Pradhan* to allocate the number of days work.

Poor women from the tribal and SC households pointed out that they still had to migrate to nearby places in search of daily wage work and said that it would be ideal if work was available to them in the vicinity of their village. Hence, the programme was not adequately addressing the needs of providing 100 days of wage work in the village, stemming migration and creating durable assets.

The labour budget was not reflecting the work demand in any of the villages/GSs visited by the team. For example, in Gaidali Nadu where there were 104 job card holders, the budget was ₹7.48 lakh as against the ideal of ₹12.48 lakh (104 job card holders × 120 × 100). It was pointed out that there was an order from the State Rural Department Ministry to reduce the labour budget. This needs to be looked into.

Wages were paid within 12 days to a fortnight though it involved costs of travel, as the bank was situated at a distance from the village. Payments through the post office (including mobile post office) were on, on a trial basis.

There has been no sample audit at the block level or a social audit by the GS. While the District Collector had visited 60 of the 160 sites of NREGS, there was a shortage of BDOs (as high as 68%) and the programme was literally being run by the *Gram Vikas Adhikari*.

Suggestions

There is a need to take stock and collect details from each department of all developmental/welfare schemes operational in the district. The next step should be to attempt convergence of multiple programmes, some of which focus on providing individual benefits and some on developing collective resources.

Convergence with forest, horticulture, animal husbandry, agriculture and other technical departments/institutions [say IARI and International Crops Research Institute for the Semi-Arid-Tropics (ICRISAT)] should be done for better shelf of projects and programme outcomes.

There is an urgent need for capacity building and training programme for all officials, programme implementation staff, PRI functionaries and community representatives on NREGS.

Fodder cultivation should be encouraged on (portion of) private land or *van panchayat* land with incentive of seed distribution from plots developed on civil-soyam land.

Why focus on Napier cultivation (green fodder)?

There is acute shortage of fodder in the mountainous State of Uttarakhand. At present, the State is in deficit of about 43.13% of dry and green fodder. According to the 2003 livestock census in the State, the fodder requirement (green and dry) for the livestock is about 197.40 lakh metric tonnes (MT) (green) and 54.31 lakh MT (dry), respectively. Hence, approximately 251.71 lakh MT of fodder is required per annum for the entire State, while the annual availability of fodder in the State is about 105.12 lakh MT (green) and 38.02 lakh MT (dry). According to the above estimates, the State has a shortage of about 108.57 lakh MT of fodder per annum. Due to scarcity of irrigation facilities, the production of green fodder is not uniform throughout the year. The availability of green fodder is only for four months (monsoon). Remaining months of the year (winter and summer), green fodder is not available resulting in low production of milk and other animal-related products. Therefore, it is important that MGNREGS allow opportunity for fodder development but not without necessary checks and balances for a sustainable and inclusive development.

Box 3.3 Napier grass and challenges of fodder devleopment in Pithoragarh

Napier grass (*Pennisetum purpureum*) is also known as 'elephant grass' which gives fodder all the year round, that is, during summer as well as winter. It was named after colonel Napier of Bulawayo in Zimbabwe who early in the last century urged the department of agriculture to explore the possibility of using it for commercial livestock production. Napier grass is a native of Rhodesia in South Africa and is cultivated in Asia, Africa, southern Europe, America, Pakistan, Sri Lanka and India. The major States in which Napier grass is grown in India are Assam, Gujarat, Madhya Pradesh, Uttar Pradesh, Punjab, West Bengal, Odisha, Bihar and Haryana.

Napier grass grows throughout the year in the tropical and sub-tropical regions. It requires warm and moist climate. The temperature range between 15°C and 30°C is suitable for its growth and development. Cold weather retards its growth; therefore, in winter its gives less cuttings than in summer.

Napier grass comes in two forms—tall and dwarf. In recent years, the dwarf 'Mott' Napier cultivar has been bred in Gainesville (Florida, USA) with a maximum height of about 1.5 m and unlike the tall variety, it is leafy and non-flowering. Tall varieties resemble sugarcane in habit. It is vegetatively propagated high-yielding perennial grass. It requires hot moist season for growth and can be grown up to an altitude of 1,500 m. Under irrigated conditions, it provides green fodder from April to November. On an average, it yields 800 quintal green fodder per hectare per year. NB-37 variety is a dwarf hybrid suitable for sub-tropical pastures. It is drought tolerant and has low oxalates (2–3%) and high crude protein (9–10%).

Climate and soil requirements for Napier

For optimal growth, Napier grass requires high and well-distributed rainfall (more than 1,000 mm per annum) although it can tolerate a moderate dry season (three to four months) because of its deep root system. At higher altitudes (above 2,100 m), growth is slowed by lower temperatures; optimal temperatures for growth are in the range 25°C to 40°C with high rainfall. It ceases to grow when temperatures fall below 10°C and the tall varieties cannot withstand frost, in contrast to the dwarf type which is frost tolerant.

Napier grass is a robust perennial bunchgrass which can form dense clumps; it has large flat leaves that may be 30–90 cm long and up to 3 cm broad. It is a shy breeding grass and seed yields are usually very low—rarely more than 1–2 kg/hectare pure germinating seed—therefore, it is usually established vegetatively from stem cuttings or crown divisions. Because the seed has low genetic stability and viability, research efforts to develop seed were shelved and seed is usually not available to farmers.

Napier grass is usually planted as a sole crop; however, it can also be under sown with other crops such as maize or intercropped with forage legumes. Because of its rapid growth and high yields, Napier grass requires regular application of nitrogen (N) phosphorus (P) and potassium (K) in the form of fertilizers or farm yard manure. Phosphorus is required at the time of planting to enable Napier grass to develop a strong root system. Later it requires nitrogen for photosynthesis. Napier grass is a heavy feeder and reduces soil nitrate, K, Ca and Mg status through nutrient uptake. The elements may be returned to the soil and taken up by other crops when Napier grass is used as mulch. Napier grass is a luxury consumer of K, far above animal requirement (0.44%) and well above the critical level (1–1.5%).

The first harvest of Napier grass should be when it attains a height of 1–1.2 m, which is usually three to four months after planting. At this stage, Napier grass has high quality and sufficient dry matter. Thereafter the grass should be harvested at intervals of six to eight weeks, when it attains the same height. To some extent, this will depend on the Napier grass variety and its ability to grow, weather conditions, soil fertility, management practices and livestock needs. If well managed, it can be harvested every month in hot and wet environments like those at the coast while during the dry season it may be harvested after two months.

Napier grass can be cultivated and its yields increase varying between 10 and 40 tonnes dry matter per hectare depending on soil fertility, climate and management factors. These yields can further be increased with usage of fertilizers and heavily irrigated and can surpass traditional grass; in the district it has potential to become main fodder crop and is fed to livestock by cut-and-carry. Research indicates that in spite of the potential for high yields, actual yields are often much lower and variable and have been measured from 2.2 to 26 tonnes dry matter per hectare per year on farms. This wide range in production is mainly caused by management factors such as the application of manure and/or fertilizer, cutting frequency and weed control.

Napier grass can grow in mixture with legumes. Although it is generally grown and managed as a pure stand, it can grow as an intercrop within the same row or within alternate rows with legumes such as *Pueraria phaseoloides*, *Centrosema pubescens*, *Neonotonia wightii*, *Desmodium uncinatum*, *Desmodium intortum* and *Stylosanthes guianensis*. When intercropped with herbaceous legumes, cutting or grazing management is adjusted to favour the legumes in order to maintain a satisfactory mixed sward. Napier grass can also be grown as an alley crop with fodder legumes such as leucaena (*Leucaena leucocephala*), calliandra (*Calliandra calothyrsus*), sesbania (*Sesbania sesban*) and gliricidia (*Gliricidia sepium*). Legumes improve the quality of Napier grass–based feed and also increase the overall yield.

In the past, Napier grass exhibited a few disease and pest incidences of economic importance and therefore a few studies addressed pests and diseases. However, in the early 1970s, a fungus causing white mould attacked the leaves and stems of most Napier grass varieties. Napier grass faces serious problems of emerging diseases, both fungal and mycoplasmal, which threaten Napier grass, and unless resistant cultivars and alternative fodders are found, the smallholder dairy industry will be in trouble. Along with the adoption problem in the local ecology, there has been mortality of the introduced Napier grasses in some of dry villages in Pithoragarh. There needs to be a search for drier varieties of grasses in these areas. Community also needs to be made aware of feeding combination of Napier with other local grasses as Napier contains oxalate which, if consumed singly, may lead to calcium deficiency in animals.

Source: A.B. Orodho, 'The role and importance of Napier grass in the smallholder dairy industry in Kenya'.

3.16 REPORT OF NATIONAL COMMITTEE FOR MGNREGS ADMINISTRATIVE AWARDS 2010–11: SALEM DISTRICT (TAMIL NADU)[19]

District profile

Salem District is located approximately midway between Bengaluru and Madurai. It is a geologist's paradise, surrounded by hills and the landscape dotted with hillocks. Yercaud, a mild-weather hill station, is an important tourism destination in the district. It is geographically divided into 19 blocks. According to the 2011 census, it has a population of 34.48 lakh. Salem has a population density of 663 inhabitants per square kilometre and literacy rate of 73.23%. Salem District is known for its mangoes, steel and Mettur dam. Mettur dam is a major source of irrigation and drinking water for Tamil Nadu.

Performance of MGNREGS in the district

In Salem District, totally 3.28 lakh job cards have been issued to households, of which 21% are SC, 6% ST and rest 67% households are others. During 2010–11, the person-days reported on the MIS dated 7 January 2012 is 125.56 lakh. On an average, 40 days of employment has been provided to SC households, 26 days to ST households and 38 days to general households. Out of the total person-days generated, women share is 87%. Only 7.7% households have completed 100 days of employment. In Tamil Nadu, every individual who has attained the age of 18 years

[19] This brief report has comments of V. Suresh Babu, Hemnath Rao and B. Panda who visited the district.

and is willing to do unskilled earthen work is provided with a job card. As noticed in other districts, the able-bodied men and women commute daily to Salem to work in garment factories, steel industry, tea processing estate, etc. and men in construction and coolie work to earn higher wages (₹300–400 per day). There is a mismatch in job cards issued for SC and ST families when compared to their households in the GP. In Gangavalli Block, two GPs were visited, viz., 74 Krishnapuram and Panchamali GP. The wage seekers informed that many of the households had not been provided with job cards and they were badly in need of them. The study team insisted on arranging job cards immediately. Accordingly, 400 job cards and 100 job cards were issued in 74 Krishnapuram and Panchamali GP, respectively. Attur Block is predominantly an agriculture-rich block. The major crops cultivated are tapioca, turmeric and paddy. Tapioca is a 10-month crop and turmeric is a nine-month crop. Per acre four to five wage seekers are required for three months in turmeric while in Tapioca 10–12 persons for four to five days per month are required. In case of paddy per acre, 7–10 wage seekers are required during the agricultural operations of sowing, weeding and harvesting. In rest of the period, family labour will take care of the agricultural operations. Hence, wage seekers are formed into groups and take up contract employment for sowing, weeding and harvesting. For example, for paddy sowing, a five-member group completes sowing of one acre paddy in half a day at a contract amount ₹2,500 to 3,000 which amounts to ₹500–600 per day. In Attur, Gangavalli, Salem, Pananmarathupatti and Veerapandy Blocks, BDOs are on the verge of retirement. Hence, they are not serious about the execution of MGNREGS works. The average wage paid under MGNREGS varies from ₹72 to ₹96 per day. *The wage seekers are not able to achieve the assigned work output as the soils are very hard. In order to achieve the assigned target by the aged and women wage seekers, it is quite essential to conduct the gender-based Time Work Motion studies. It is also necessary to provide women-friendly tools to achieve the assigned task.* The malnourished and lactating women are not able to work efficiently with crowbar weighing 8 kg and small-sized spades.

In Ramakrishna Palayam, Attur Block, Kulla Punnu Raja, holding job card no. 290708140625 aged 45 years, belonging to the SC community, has worked for 44 days. He is basically a farmer cultivating turmeric and paddy. He informed that turmeric is an one-year crop while paddy is a 150-day crop. The net profit per acre from turmeric is around ₹20,000 and from paddy it is ₹10,000 after deducting the actual expenditure. He used to pay ₹100 for men and ₹70 for women before MGNREGS. The wages have slightly increased after the execution of MGNREGS (men ₹120 and women ₹100 per day). As a farmer, he is not ready to pay higher and equal wages for men and women. The contract labour is preferred for agricultural operations such as sowing, weeding and harvesting. On contract, ₹2,000 is paid for four persons per acre per day.

In Veerapandy Block, the cash book is entered using pencil. The BDO has not verified any records. In Pananamarathu Patti Block, Kuralnatham GP, Jarugumalai village tribal habitation, there is no approach road to the village. The work was sanctioned without visiting the site by the BDO, Secretary or Assistant Executive Engineer. Based on the report provided by the overseer and Panithala Porupalayar (worksite facilitators), the road work is sanctioned without proper technical survey. In none of the works, the team could locate the cross-section diagram of the project. In many of the visited GPs, the pre-, mid- and post-photographs are not affixed. In none of the GPs, asset register is available.

In Salem Block, men get easy employment in saw mills. In Salem Block alone, there are 90 saw mills and Timber mart. The women wage seekers requested to suggest the government to increase the maximum number of days of work from 100 to at least 150 days. Fifty per cent of their MGNREGS wages are spent on consumption of food, 30% on transport and grocery, 10% on medicine and 10% on saving. It was informed by the wage seekers that if the number of days was increased by additional 50 days, the additional wages earned could be invested on their children's education. Presently they are depending on the free government education.

Wages are being paid based on the overall work output generated per week by the wage seekers. Measurement is not done group-wise.

Affirmative action to enhance the participation of marginalized community

The State operational guidelines do not permit any individual works, material component and more than one work per GP under MGNREGS. However, presently, the State has considered forming the wage seekers into clusters and providing employment near their habitat under the cluster approach. According to the MIS data as on 7 January 2012, during 2010–11, the work status report indicates that only three works are shown as completed. All the three works are executed under Category VIII (rural connectivity). About 2,898 works are shown as ongoing/suspended works. It indicates that the MIS data are not updated.

Grievance redressal mechanism

Social audit has been conducted twice a year. However, no social audit report is available at the GP level for verification. Complaint register has been maintained; perhaps no complaints have been received at the GP and block levels. When enquired with the wage seekers, none of them is familiar with the toll-free complaint number. This indicates that the GRM is not effective.

Good practices

As such the team could not find any innovative or good practices in Salem District. The measurement sticks have been provided to the working groups, in order to measure their work output on a particular day. For example, a person has to dig 2 m length × 1 m width × 0.6 m depth earth for a day's work. For the benefit of the wage seeker, three sticks measuring the desired depth (0.6 m), width (1.0 m) and length (2.0 m) for easy measurement are provided.

Other observations

General performance

Since work on improving individual land is not permitted under the guidelines of the Tamil Nadu Government, most of the works carried out in Salem District under MGNREGA relate either to road connectivity or to development of community assets such as water tanks and supply and drainage channels. It was found in most villages that job cards have been selectively issued and very few families have completed 100 days of work in relation to the total number of rural households in the GPs visited during the field visits. Presidents and members of the GPs showed low levels of awareness about MGNREGS which was even less among wage seekers. The average wage was around ₹100 and in some villages such as Masikalaiyur habitation of Gonur GP, it was observed that as many as 200 households were yet to receive job cards despite repeated requests by the wage seekers. Attendance in the GS was quite low.

Asset quality

A large number of works encompassing either desilting of ponds or excavation of new ponds seem to have been initiated long after technical and financial sanctions were received with the consequence that there was cost overrun and the same projects were continuing in the succeeding year without reviewing and resubmitting the project proposals for revision of cost. Where the works were completed, the quality of asset was either unsatisfactory in execution or poorly maintained. However, it was noted that the impact of the programme was not entirely lost since in one GP

(Olaipatti) of Macheri Block, 69 acres of land was additionally irrigated through deepening and lengthening of a supply channel connecting the major irrigation tank of the village. There was no evidence of any focussed effort to address the economic interests of SC or ST farmers through MGNREGA works.

The average wage hovered around ₹100 per day and the proportion of families completing 100 days of employment was consistently low across all the GPs visited. There was often a mismatch between the numbers of days of work completed as per the employment registers and the data updated on the job cards. The training of the presidents and other office bearers of GPs is an urgent necessity since their understanding of the MGNREGA processes and workers' rights was very poor. The low level of wages combined with the State guidelines on implementing only one work at a time in the GP has proved ineffective in checking migration and at the same time resulted in serious problems of inter-habitation equity. Some GPs have more than a dozen habitations, all of them eagerly looking for works to be implemented in their own hamlet.

There was also no evidence of any significant innovation either in the choice of works or implementation processes. On the positive side, the availability of the GP level data was found to be reasonably good.

Five blocks were visited—Valapadi, Peddnaickanpalayam, Sankari, Konganapuram and Magudanchavadi in Salem District of Tamil Nadu on 24th and 25th of December 2011. The GPs visited in these blocks are Neermulikutai and Puluthikuttai in Vlapadi Block, Edyapatti and Pappanaickanpatti in Peddnaickanpalayam Block, Katheri and Morur West in Sankari Block, Thangayur in Konganapuram Block and Vaikundam in Magudanchavadi Block. The team visited nine ongoing work sites and had direct interaction with workers. The team also visited four completed works and had interaction with workers and other stakeholders.

Nirmullikuttai GP

In Nirmullikuttai GP, (i) application and job card issue register, (ii) receipt and expenditure register, (iii) household employment register, (iv) job card stock register (v) nominal muster roll resister and (vi) GS register were examined. Records were well kept.

Worksite: One ongoing work 'Desilting Panathoppu Southside and Deepening of Pond' was visited. Here 37 workers were working, out of which 36 were women and 31 were from SC community. Gender aspect is well taken care of. However, shade and crèche are not provided. First-aid box is there. The team checked the job cards (random sample job card nos. 0226B, 0226A, 0439A, 0440 B and 0436B)

and found them up to date. The quality of the asset created does not impress the team. Payment is made within eight days on the designated pay day, i.e. Tuesday of the week.

Equity: Gender and social equity is taken care of in terms of participation of women and SC workers in MGNREGA work. However, inter-habitation equity remains a problem area.

Capacity building: Capacity building is average; it needs improvement. Social hierarchy still affects the outcome of MGNREGA. Team spirit is absent.

Work type: The State Government has put restriction on the number of works to be undertaken. The work undertaken involves digging of hard soil and the payment is made on outturn basis. Since the soil is very hard, the female workers get, on an average, ₹60 for a seven-hour work.

Puluthikuttai GP

In Puluthikuttai GP, record keeping was examined of (i) application and job card issue register, (ii) receipt and expenditure register, (iii) household employment register, (iv) job card stock register, (v) nominal muster roll resister and (vi) GS register. Records were well kept.

Worksite: One ongoing work was visited. About 143 workers were found to be working including 141 women, 139 from ST community, two from SC community and one from OBC. Gender aspect is well taken care of. However, shade and crèche are not provided. First aid is there. Payment is made within eight days on the designated pay day, i.e. Tuesday of the week.

Equity: Gender and social equity is taken care of in terms of participation of women and ST workers in MGNREGA work. However, inter-habitation equity remains a problem area.

Capacity building: Capacity building is average which needs improvement. Team spirit is absent.

PRI participation: The last GS was held on 15 August 2011 and the resolution of this GS was signed by a handful of workers.

Edyapatti GP

In Edyapatti GP, record keeping examined was of: (i) application and job card issue register, (ii) receipt and expenditure register, (iii) household employment register, (iv) job card stock register, (v) nominal muster oll register and (vi) GS register. Records are well kept.

Worksite: The team visited one ongoing work and checked the job cards. The entries in the job card match the entries in the NMR. Gender aspect is well taken care of. However, shade and crèche are not provided. First aid is there. Payment is made within eight days on the designated pay day, i.e. Tuesday of the week.

Demand for work: An analysis of the total number of households registered for work and the total number of man-days generated in 2010–11 shows extremely low demand for MGNREGS work. Even for SC/ST households, the situation is not better. The total number of ST households registered for work in this GP was 256 in 2010–11, whereas the total number of ST man-days generated was 392, which means in the whole year 2010–11, employment demanded/provided per ST was less than two man-days.

Equity: Gender and social equity is taken care of in terms of participation of women and ST workers in MGNREGA work.

Capacity building: Capacity building is average which needs improvement. Team spirit is absent. Leadership from the PRI functionaries and PO is lacking.

Vaikundam GP

In Vaikundam GP, the demand process in this GP is imperfect and full of distortions. Element of exclusion is very much visible. There has not been any kind of mobilization to capture demand. A number of old and poor people who are drawing old-age pension are denied work in MGNREGA on the plea that they are drawing old-age pension. Further, on house-to-house enquiry, it was found that there were individuals who wanted work but were not provided the same/not registered. P. Kandhaswamy has demanded a job card but has not been provided with the same. Chellama Amma requires work but has not been given a job card.

Record keeping: Record keeping is imperfect. In MGR Nagar, 48 persons were registered in 2008 but the data were not entered in the MIS.

Worksite: The team visited one ongoing work and checked the job cards. The entries in the job cards in few cases do not match the entries in the NMR. No sign board/work board was found. Payment is made within eight days on the designated pay day, i.e. Tuesday of the week. Crèche and shade are not provided.

Equity: Gender and social equity is taken care of in terms of participation of women and ST workers in MGNREGS work.

Thangayur GP

In Thangayur GP, the demand registration process was flawed and distorted. There is demand for job cards but these are not issued by the *panchayat*. Cards were in stock but not issued to people who demanded it. Kaveriyammal and Karuppan had applied for job cards but were not given the same for the last one year. Six women workers complained that they were willing to work but were not given job cards.

Record keeping: Record keeping was unsatisfactory. The GS register was not properly maintained. GS resolution was recorded in respect of a few meetings.

Pencil entries were made in many registers which raised suspicion.

Participation: Participation is skewed as the president has an upper cast bias. GS is called without adequate prior information.

Capacity building: Capacity building is poor. There is a computer in the GP office but it remains unused. Sense of involvement at every level is visible.

Equity: Inter-habitation equity in demand and work is not taken care of. Exclusion is visible.

Positivities

Overall the positive factors were

(i) Payment is made within eight days on the designated pay day, i.e. Tuesday of the week.
(ii) Women and ST workers in many GPs predominate MGNREGA work.

Deficiencies

The following deficiencies are noticed:

(i) The demand registration situation is flawed and sub-optimal. Exclusion is clearly visible in some of the GPs. In certain cases, the exclusion is deliberate and is the result of the landlord hegemony.
(ii) Worksite facilities such as shade and crèche are not available.
(iii) Inter-habitation equity is not taken care of.
(iv) Participation of workers in decision making is skewed in some *panchayat*s.
(v) There is not much of convergence with line departments.
(vi) There is limitation of two works per GP.
(vii) Habitation-wise data of jobseekers are not available.

3.17 REPORT OF NATIONAL COMMITTEE FOR MGNREGS ADMINISTRATIVE AWARDS 2010–11: SARGUJA DISTRICT (CHHATTISGARH)[20]

In Premnagar and Surajgad Blocks, there is good enthusiasm and synergy among the younger people working on MGNREGS and at the field extension level. Also, there is a growing number of women field staff. They are young and interested in showcasing their work. However, the engineers, being seniors in age and higher in the bureaucratic hierarchy, seem to dominate the process whose perception of

---

[20] This report has comments of K.S. Gopal and G.N. Sharma who visited the district. Please see the summary and theme-wise reports for comments of K.B. Saxena.

'worker' as *kamchor* biases the entire team and leads to extracting more work in difficult circumstances. It has also led to an overall thinking of traditional 'work types and approaches' being preferred. These engineers are all retired officials.

All households have job cards. Officials and field staff understand that their task is to ensure delivering 100 days of work. A decent percentage of households have completed 100 days of work and a good number of households are in the above 50 days employment provisioning. The team found more of men than women at work and in some instances equal number of both. This seems different from what one sees in other States. Whether this is because of the type of works being taken up or the period when this visit was undertaken or the culture in the area is not verifiable, except from data. Thus, work provisioning here must be applauded and recognized. This is also because the relationship of the field staff with the community is good and they have motivated the *sarpanch*s in many places to play an active role.

Water is provided at worksites but there are no shades and first-aid boxes, and nowhere does one see a crèche. Some equity can be seen as workers are tribals. Water conservation is high on priority and water is abundant and this is being harnessed well in tanks and used for fishing, etc. It will be good if water management can also be promoted along with better farming practices so that this resource can make a considerable impact on their incomes.

The works taken up are, as already stated, handicapped by aged engineers with a regulated bias and it is important that promotion of 'development' and 'livelihood' has centrality rather than checks and measurements in the implementation process. Also the material component in roads is high because funds are being used for roads and culverts which are much needed here. However, the district receives funds from multiple sources such as BRGF and *Vishesh Kendra Sahayata*. How these funds are used in a convergent mode cannot be analyzed as such data for one project are not available at one point. On this aspect, the district head does not seem to have given any attention. This has also led to some wasteful investment such as a brick wall fencing (₹1,800) for trees planted rather than bush fencing with forest species such as glyrecidia that are not browsed by cattle.

Another aspect which could not be investigated is the source from which construction material is procured for schemes. The materials such as stone or bricks though available locally are sourced from far-away places where, the team understands, syndicates operate. This has implications for cost and quality of materials besides corrupt practices occurring in procurement process. The team is of the view that the MoRD must take a view on such practices being adopted by the State Government and ensure that as far as possible materials are locally purchased. It is important that the poor quality material is not used leading to poor life of the asset being built.

Overall the team would say that this district has done reasonable well. But it need not be considered as LWA as the area the team visited does not face Naxalite violence in any serious way. But the state must do better planning when it comes to work, optimize the benefits from resources being developed (next stage of extension activities must be provided) and above all the officials must help workers by providing them good quality instruments as they are using very blunted digging shovels leading to unnecessary hard work and if this is what the team saw during winter, one can imagine what the plight of workers would be in summer when most MGNREGS works are to be taken up.

In short, the performance of the district is good in provisioning of work, reaching out beneficiaries and community relations. It is just about okay (considering its immediate past performance and being an area that is somewhat difficult to reach and has received few government schemes) in compliance of procedures to ensure that all rights are delivered and provisions under the Act are observed including aspects such as social audit and transparency and in the type of works being taken up. But the district is weak and does not seem to have applied much attention to planning and delivering better and more optimal results on the works being taken up or in exploring new ideas and pathways to augment development benefits through convergence.

Finally, having seen other areas and considering the backdrop in which this district is placed, it has done quite well and needs to be recognized. However, one cannot deem this as innovative or pioneering or a model in any manner. The overall performance can be termed as efficient delivery but it is falling short on effective and creative implementation of the Act.

3.18 REPORT OF NATIONAL COMMITTEE FOR MGNREGS ADMINISTRATIVE AWARDS 2010–11: THRISSUR DISTRICT (KERALA)[21]

District profile

Thrissur District is situated in the central part of Kerala. It has 17 blocks, 92 GPs and 254 villages. It is home to over 10% of the Kerala's population. According to the 2011 census, the district population

---

[21] This brief report has comments of V. Suresh Babu, Reetika Khera and K.B. Saxena who visited the district.

is about 31.1 lakh with a density of 1,026 inhabitants per square kilometre. Its literacy rate is around 92.56% which is much higher than the national average. The rural BPL families are around 2.25 lakh. Thrissur is known for the power loom industry and the textile mills (hosiery products). Also, the coir and the tile industry offers employment for many people in the district. Most of the timber is brought down from the forests to Thrissur and Chalakkudy, which are the most important timber marts in the district. The match-stick industry, pharmaceuticals, printing, etc. give Thrissur its fame as a bustling industrial centre.

Performance of MGNREGS in the district

The district has registered 2.50 lakh households under MGNREGS covering 3.95 lakh wage seekers. In total, 2.49 lakh individual job cards were issued. During 2010–11, MGNREGS provided employment to 36.7% of households having job cards, 24.5% persons of registered job seekers and generated 40.73 lakh person-days. About 11,000 families completed 100 days of employment.

Out of total 2.49 lakh job cards, 16.8% belong to SCs, 0.66% to STs and the rest to 'others' category. A total of 40.73 lakh person-days were generated of which 25.8% was the share of SCs, 0.51% of STs and 95.6% of women wage seekers. However, during visits to the GPs, it was found that there was demand for job cards as well as employment by the members of disadvantaged sections. The number of job cards issued to the disadvantaged section households is not in conformity with the actual number (total) of households. The demand for MGNREGS is very high.

The district administration has insisted on GRSs to conduct a 'project meeting'—an innovative system to create awareness among wage seekers with regard to project details, mobilize and collect demand from interested wage seekers as also to brief them on their rights and entitlements prior to initiation of the project. The wage seekers take an oath to complete the project in the assigned duration and maintain unity among wage seekers to achieve the desired work output and integrity of the project. The GRS has to maintain the site dairy, which includes attendance of wage seekers (who take the oath) and a check-list containing 17 items to be carried out during the project period. In case an MGNREGS project needs to be executed on an individual land, the beneficiary has to produce possession certificate with regard to land.

In Pazhayannur GP, it was found that only few registers were being maintained under MGNREGS such as those relating to issue of job cards, issue of cheques, technical sanction, stock, social audit, shelf of projects and assets. In the asset register, pre-, mid- and post-project photographs were not affixed. It was surprising to learn that wage seekers were not provided with bank passbook. The wages earned by the wage seeker is entered in the job card itself. For instance, job card of Pramila w/o Balakrishna (job card no. KL-07-013-005-004/5) indicates that she worked for a total of 108 days from 2008–09 to 2011–12. The wages were drawn from Punjab National Bank.

In the same GP, works undertaken were of land development (for cultivation of banana, ginger, turmeric, colacasia and elephant corn), renovation of water bodies, water conservation and harvesting, irrigation canal, individual works on SC/ST land, flood control (clearing aquatic weeds in drains and canals) and rural connectivity. Agricultural employment is seasonal and available only during the months of June–August and December. The market wages (for women ₹200 per day and for men ₹300–400 per day) are higher than the MGNREGS wages. Able-bodied men (of 20–45 years) do not participate in MGNREGS, as the wages on offer are only ₹150. Women employed during the harvesting season are provided with one *para* paddy which is approximately 15 kg (the value of which is around ₹150). There is no proper assessment of work output for calculation of wage under MGNREGS; hence full wages are paid. It is informed that the engineers consider the total output generated in a week and average wage is computed on this basis and paid.

Affirmative action to enhance the participation of marginalized community

The district completed 10,317 MGNREGS works during the financial year 2010–11. Of these, 27% of works related to flood control, 18% to traditional water bodies, 16% to land development, 15% to water conservation and harvesting, 9% to irrigation canals and 8% to affirmative works. The types of works executed are mostly related to plantation, land levelling and preparation of ground for agriculture or vegetable cultivation, soil and moisture conservation works under coconut plantation, casuarina plantation along the coast line (green belt to prevent salinity/sea water ingress/protection against sea storm), cleaning of drains, clearing of aquatic weeds and construction of roads or improvement of roads.

In case of SC and ST individual lands, very limited land is available (on an average, three to four cents per household) for development. In order to extend land development projects for SC and ST families, seed materials of turmeric, ginger, banana are provided to encourage their cultivation in kitchen gardens to ensure livelihoods and increase their purchasing power. The works taken up under MGNREGS is mostly carried out in APL land holdings. Weeding/land preparation for cultivation of vegetables and in coconut orchards is one of the works executed under MGNREGS. In such works, a wage seeker has to cover an area of three cents or 120 sq. m per day. Mud pasting of the boundary bunds of an SC/ST household is also considered for MGNREGS work in which about 16 m length × 30 cm height × 40–50 cm width has to be achieved per day per person to draw full wage.

MGNREGS works taken up in the district are not very appropriate and durable. However, in Kadapuram GP, Chavakadu Block, casuarina plantation has been taken up across a 9 km coastal belt in a phased manner. The survival rate is very impressive. *The district administration should lay emphasis on creating durable and quality assets under MGNREGS.*

Grievance redressal mechanism

In Chelakkara GP, it was noticed that six complaints were registered under MGNREGS. All of them were filed due to political rivalry, and subsequently cleared. Social audit is organized twice a year. There was no complaint registered during social audit. Complaint box is noticed in all the GPs. However, no complaints had been received. Toll-free number has been displayed on all the notice boards. It indicates that the wage seekers and the village community are happy with the process of execution.

Good practices

In the GPs, the team could find one good practice, that is, awareness is not a one-time affair. As and when a new project is initiated, a project meeting is conducted by the GRS. The mate mobilizes the entire village community to attend the meeting. During the meeting, the GRS and the mate provide a brief on the project details and collect the demand from wage seekers. Before commencement of the project, 17 items of action are to be taken such as preparing the GRS regarding minutes of the meeting, awareness generation on quantum of work to be done to earn full wage, formation of groups, time of completion, project cost, working hours, filling muster roll, etc. *Apart from project meeting, measurement sticks are given to the wage groups to know the quantum of work generated.* No other innovation has been noticed in the GPs visited.

Other observations

In the district, there were very limited avenues for taking up NREGS work. In addition, the schemes taken up were of very short duration. Several schemes such as field preparation, vegetable farming, coconut bed preparation and drain cleaning did not qualify to be NREGS works.

There were no norms of work for payment, nor a piece rate based on actual output of work. Daily attendance (twice a day) was required to earn a day's wages.

Records, mainly the maintenance of various registers at the GP/block level, were updated in most of the districts.

The team saw MGNREGS workers wrongfully digging out top soil from adjacent agricultural fields (which belonged to tribals or SCs) during construction of earthen bunds and agriculture field roads. In fact, at one place the officials defended it saying that owner's consent had been taken and it was being done to deepen the field of that person without realizing its adverse impact on the fertility of the soil.

In the name of convergence, subsidy was being provided to big farmers and landholders. In fact, it was brought to the team's notice (Edavaialgu GP) that the APL families too were getting NREGS job cards made, to take advantage of NREGS subsidy in preparing fields for vegetable cultivation. While the money for digging work came from NREGS funds, the agriculture department was providing the seeds.

A good practice of financial management observed was that overhead balance was not allowed to be accumulated at the GP level. Unspent/unused money did not stay with the *panchayat*. However, in quite a few GPs the team saw instances of huge difference in the budget proposed in the annual action plan (AAP) and money actually spent. It was not clear whether the district or the block received money from the MoRD on the basis of the AAP and if there was overhead balance at the block or district level.

During the team's conversations at Panacherry GP office it was observed that there were only two staff members per GP for all NREGS activities. They were dependent on other line department officials for excluding work. For example, the agriculture officer was the authorized official for approving completion of work. This led to delay in payment of wages.

Mobilization of SC/ST labour was being done through SC/ST promoters which facilitated landless SCs/STs demanding and participating in MGNREGS work.

In Vellukara village, women workers working on a drain (leading to irrigation channel) cleaning work told the team that on an average 15–20 days in a month, both men and women were without work, hence without income.

Overall, person-days of work generated was low as also the fact that most NREGS works undertaken were largely of short durations, say of around two weeks. In Thamarachaal, a tribal village and a single-crop area, a total of only 19 days of work had been provided during 2011–12. As against work demanded, work provision was very low. For instance, one woman worker had demanded 14 days of work during June–July against which only three days of work had been provided. Payments in passbooks reflected work for merely two weeks for the entire team (which were in one go). People here were in urgent need of work.

In Taamravaylachaar village of Panacherry GP, where people were agitating for provision of NREGS work, job cards showed three to four days of work for the entire year. For this village, which had 209 job cards, the average days of work provided per person during 2010–11 was 6.09 days. In the same year, while it had a budget of ₹88 lakh, only ₹58 lakh were spent, implying 40% unspent money.

One could sense that genuine demand for work was getting suppressed. In Thrissur, the team was told, nearly 60% job cards had been slashed in 2011–12—either cancelled or not renewed. This included omission of SCs and STs. In Vellangalur Block (which had four villages including Vellukura which had a higher share of SCs and STs and Kottanool), nearly 75% job cards had been done away with. While the number of job cards was 2,848 in 2010–11, it was reduced to 799 in 2011–12.

Field visit experience was contrary to official records which indicated that people demanding employment under NREGS were very few and potential of demand was very low. Records suggested that only 25% of people were demanding work, which seemed incorrect going by what people told the team and required further investigation. In fact, in Vellukura, the number of job card holders (799) almost matched with the number of persons who demanded work (743), indicating suppressed demand.

It was told by a block-level official that the measurement of agriculture-related works under NREGS had to be approved/signed by the agriculture officer, which invariably took time, causing at least a month's delay in payment of wage labour. Wage delay had two important ramifications: it discouraged participation in NREGS works and forced the labourer to opt for work which provided far less wages but on time.

Across blocks, 'land development' works had been taken up on a considerable scale. Many of such works (undertaken in collaboration with the agriculture department), however, were clearly agriculture work on private lands, such as mud-mound preparation for coconut cultivation and preparing five cents of land for kitchen garden. These were clearly a violation of the NREGS.

Another issue that came to the team's notice was in Chandrapini village (Edathiruthy GP) pertained to reclaiming of a 3.5 hectare land (owned by a well-off person) lying fallow for 20 years, by engaging NREGS workers. To put paperwork in place, a one-year land lease agreement between the owner and a women's SHG group of 20 women workers had been made, whereby the latter could take up agricultural activities for generating income. This had the consent of the *panchayat*. Under Kutumbshree, the SHG would be entitled to subsidies (of seed, fertilizer, etc.) and loan for agricultural operations. An investment of ₹20,000 would supposedly yield a return of ₹40,000, the team was told. This was a smart ploy for not only reclaiming long-unused fallow land of a rich farmer, but making it an agriculture-worthy and profitable asset through government subsidy. The terms of lease and rent charges were not known.

In fact, a lot of land development was being done on land owned by APL families. Their inclusion was being justified by categorizing them as small and marginal farmers. An interesting argument given in the district was that public/government land was not available, thereby forcing *panchayats* to undertake NREGS works on private lands. *This was almost a misuse of Central Government funds and there needs to be a rethink on allowing transfer of NREGS funds for such activities.*

In several *panchayats* in Thrissur, the number of days worked by women as reflected in the MIS and what the women actually reported during conversations pointed out to a large gap. Possibly, incorrect data were being fed into the MIS. This aspect needs further validation.

In Eriad (GP), a coastal area village in Thrissur, affected by tsunami a few years ago, under NREGS work, a wall of sand-filled plastic sacks was being erected to reduce the force of waves and prevent sea water ingress into the village. The utility of such work was suspect as the sand wall would be no match for the force and height of sea water waves and would get washed off during high tide. A better idea would have been to treat this space by a boulder-protection wall (which already exists in patches).

The nature of schemes taken under NREGS did not add up to something substantial. Small-duration works (schemes) were taken which hardly lasted a week or so. Some did not qualify for NREGS works. Say for instance, canal cleaning was more like cleaning of drains running in front of houses. Rather than any desilting work, it was simply removal of grass.

No trace of agricultural land could be seen nearby. Similarly preparing five cents of land of kitchen garden and mound preparation for coconut plantations were doubtful works. In fact, no permanent asset was being created.

Massive participation of women in NREGA was observed. Not only on the worksites but also at almost every conceivable post such as assistant engineers, overseers, data entry operators, *panchayat* presidents, mates and BDOs, women were to be seen in position. The 'skill ladder' exists in some positions.

GPs have a strong role in planning and implementation process. PRIs are very strong, with amazing infrastructure (GP offices resemble block offices of some of the northern States), and everything goes through them. They actually seem to prepare annual plans for each *panchayat* and follow the prioritization decided in the GS. The block *panchayat* has standing committees on different subjects. The blocks that were visited often had various block *panchayat* members who were there because they were expecting a visitor from Delhi; it seems that they are always around.

A demand-driven process seemed to be in place, at least partially. There is an application window at the *panchayat* office to receive applications. However, unemployment allowance is not paid. Awareness on this was also low.

One of the team members felt that convergence in asset creation was (with some caveats) truly a remarkable feature of NREGS here. With Kudumbashree taking a massive interest in NREGS, every possible kind of convergence was taking place. The cattle breeding farm under the Veterinary University offers their land to NREGS labourers to work for growing fodder for the cattle.

Canal maintenance and sluice gate maintenance were the other big works. In the district, desilting of canals facilitates its utilization for irrigation purposes, and also raises the water level in private wells.

Delays in payment of wages continue to be a problem, though not at all like in the northern States. Here payments were made in 20–25 days, according to district officials, who were quite candid about it. It appeared that delays were at two stages. First, submission of paperwork by the mate to the GP and second, cross measurement by the assistant engineer.

Other observations

In the category of private works permissible for small/marginal farmers, private works are being taken up on the farms of people who definitely are not below poverty line. One of the farms visited by the team was that of a film director.

There was a private college for which NREGS funds were spent in land levelling and water conservation works including forestry. It is hardly a public asset.

Wages are high. Menfolk do not participate in NREGS works as the wages in the market are much higher than NREGS wages. SHGs are the organizations which take up the work on private lands. NREGS works are not taken up when farming activity is there even if there is demand of work. Records are not maintained with reference to work demand and its provisioning. The records show that demand and start of the work match finely. That is why no unemployment allowance has been paid even in a single case in the district.

There are case studies of positive impacts of NREGS. Here is one small example of a group in Pariyaram GP (Chalakudy Block, Thrissur).

The group consisted of about 15 workers, with two men and a female mate. All except one had worked about 40 days on NREGA in the past year. The only exception was a slightly elderly woman who had started working this year.

What did they do with their money? Omana Hamsa (worked 40 days last financial year) bought sand to renovate her house; Jayathi (48 days) did house repairs, Shaila Sadanan (35 days) bought gold for her children; Shirley Sunderesan (35) used it to repay Kudumbashree linkage loan of ₹50,000 from bank for house; Kamalam Revi (25 days) and Sheela Balu (35 days) who had bought a cow on a Kudumbashree loan are repaying this with their NREGA earning; Anitha Sajinan (45 days) used it for her daughter's college education and the mate Jancy Balan (52 days) used it to pay her son's computer course fee plus her house loan; Vinayan (35 days) used it to repay house loan that his mother took four years ago; Kuttan (35 days) bought himself a gold ring.

3.19 REPORT OF NATIONAL COMMITTEE FOR MGNREGS ADMINISTRATIVE AWARDS 2010–11: VIZIANAGARAM DISTRICT (ANDHRA PRADESH)[22]

District profile

Vizianagaram district extended over an area of 6,539 sq. km, covering 1,551 villages (1,524 are rural villages). The total number of households in

---

[22] This brief report has comments of V. Suresh Babu and B. Panda who visited the district. Please see the summary and theme-wise reports for comments of K.B. Saxena.

the district is 5.15 lakh and the sex ratio is 1,009. Out of the total workers (11.75 lakh), cultivators are 3.31 lakh (28%), agricultural labourers are 4.71 lakh (40%), household industry workers are 0.43 lakh (4%) and other workers are 3.27 lakh (28%). The SC and ST population in the district is around 11% and 9%, respectively. The rural population in the district is about 82%. There are 34 *mandal*s in the district. For administrative convenience, the district is divided into two revenue divisions, viz., Vizianagaram (plains) and Parvathipuram (hilly region). The average rainfall of the district is 1,131 mm per annum. The agency area of Parvathipuram division covers seven *mandal*s. The gross area irrigated during *kharif* is 1.21 lakh acres while in *rabi* 0.33 lakh acres. Paddy is the major crop during *kharif* season. Maize and Finger millet are cultivated during *rabi*.

Performance of MGNREGS in the district

Vizianagaram District has provided 4.96 lakh job cards with 12% each to SCs and STs. Overall, 219.06 lakh person-days of employment were generated during the previous year, from which 13% SCs, 14% STs, 73% others and 58% women were benefitted. On an average, SC households were provided with 48 days, ST with 50 days and in general 44 days of employment per household.

The process of executing MGNREGS is reasonably good. The demand dated acknowledgement slips were provided to the wage seekers. The SSSs are nothing but a group of 10–20 household working members who come together to demand employment and work under MGNREGS. They unanimously elect the group leader who is known as mate. The role of the mate is to take attendance on the muster roll, provide pre-marking of site to the wage seeker, educate and create awareness on the quantum of work to be completed to earn the prescribed minimum wage. He is paid ₹2 per member of his group. He also educates the wage seekers who give thumb impression on the muster roll. Hence, he is also known as *vidya* mate. Being a *vidya* mate, he can earn ₹90 as an incentive per illiterate wage seeker in a period of three months. Fifty per cent of the amount (i.e. ₹45) is paid in the initial month and another 50% is paid after the wage seeker gets through the written exam. In Vizianagaram District, there are 31,540 SSSs. About 98.13% of individuals who demand work participate in it. About 92,847 families have completed 100 days.

In an SSS group, a maximum of four members can get their crowbar and earn additional amount of ₹5 per day. While other women members are provided ₹3 for bringing their baskets. Each wage seeker is also paid ₹1.25 per day for bringing his/her drinking water. During winter months, ₹1.25 per litre is paid while ₹2.50 is paid during summer months for this purpose. *However, no tool sharpening charges are paid for the implements used to clear the bushes (for example, sickles, axes, choppers, etc.).*

Under the land development programme, 91,442 acres of land was brought under cultivation. Near about 17,573 acres of right of first refusal land has been developed. Around 6,000 acres of land has been planted with mango, cashewnut, etc.

As a State Government initiative, each *mandal* has three to four nurseries maintained by the MGNREGS wage seekers with the technical support of the forest department. Near about 53 lakh seedlings were raised in 104 nurseries. About 32 lakh teak and 12 lakh non-teak seedlings have been planted on field bunds. As a result of convergence with the minor irrigation department, approximately 10,500 tanks have been desilted and bunds were strengthened. Due to revival of traditional water bodies, the water table has reportedly risen to 2.45 m in last 5 years. The area under irrigated *rabi* cultivation has increased. *A systematic study needs to be conducted to verify the claims and document the impact of MGNREGS. None of the physically challenged wage seekers is paid 30% additional wages.* Aam Admi Bima *and* Swasthya Bima Yojana *are not provided to the wage seekers.*

Affirmative action to enhance the participation of marginalized community

The district has developed 91,716 acres of SC, ST, and small and marginal farmers' land and brought it under cultivation. Three community irrigation wells have been excavated in Badangi *mandal*. A cluster of 10 acres of cultivable SC/ST land is provided with a community irrigation well. As a result of the community well, the cropping system has changed especially in *rabi* season. The area under irrigation of SC/ST land has increased. Area under floriculture has also increased on the lands of the SCs, STs and small and marginal farmers. When such initiatives were nonexistent, the members of the disadvantaged section used to migrate to the command areas such as East and West Godavari District as contract labourers. The contractors provided ₹6,000 for a period of three months with free board and lodging facilities. Fifty per cent of the amount is paid in advance. Hence, the landless labourers in the age group of 15–45 years still prefer the contractor employment, which promotes high women participation. This needs to be verified. Due to increase in the income levels of the SC/ST and small and marginal farmers of Therlam *mandal*, they are able to educate their children in technical courses (BE). Alajangi Nagaiah having job card no. 10080 is educating his son A. Kamalakar for Mechanical Engineering in PITS engineering college, Gangaiahpeta, Krishna District. Yandava Latchayya, job card no. 10018, is educating his son Y. Pratap for engineering in Gokul College, Bobbili *mandal*, Vizianagaram District.

There is a one-month delay in disbursement of wages to the wage seekers. The delay is mainly due to the postal department procedures and lack of staff at the BPO level. Though the funds are released to the sub-post office (SPO), without approval of the district post, master pay order cannot be sanctioned by the SPO to disburse the wages by the BPO.

Application of IT has affected the updating of job cards and book keeping at the GP level as the pay slips issued to the wage seekers contain all the information, for example, wage details, number of days left to complete 100 days and other allowances such as drinking water and implement sharpening charges.

Grievance redressal mechanism

Social audit has been conducted three times in this year, and the fourth social audit campaign is under process. The findings of the social audit are being followed up by stringent action. In compilation of social audit findings, several officials and grassroots level workers have been suspended/removed from the service. The findings made with regard to misappropriations were acted upon by recovering the excess expenditure. Overall, only 0.24% deviation from the norms has been pointed out in the social audit.

Good practices

Except for State initiatives such as Electronic Muster Roll Management System, Electronic Measurement System and Central Fund Management System, not much district intervention in respect of innovation and good practices is noticed.

Other observations

Four *manadal*s and seven GPs in this district were visited including five worksites. Performance of this district on the ground is very satisfactory.

Positives/achievements

Social audit has been done regularly and action taken on its findings also finds a place in the register.

Record keeping is excellent. The following registers were maintained in every *mandal* that was visited.

1. Muster roll watch register
2. Grievance register,
3. Internal audit register
4. FTO register
5. Review meeting register
6. Movement register
7. BPM meeting register
8. Error register
9. Muster status register
10. Stock register
11. Wage FTO register
12. *Palli Sabha* register (GP level)
13. RTI register

Demand process is near perfect. Exclusion is minimal.

Social and gender equity is adhered to perfectly in MGNREGS work.

Monitoring and evaluation is one of the best the team has seen.

Reasonable degree of capacity building has been done in terms of training of the field assistants, mates, APOs and MPDOs.

Transparency level in the implementation process is good. All works undertaken, job card holders who worked and the number of days they worked are mentioned on the walls of visible places in large letters for public display.

One of the best innovations and convergences that the district has done is linking up this programme with the National Literacy Mission (*Sikhya Bharati*). Under this programme, each literate mate is given an incentive of ₹1 per person to make workers literate by taking group classes in the evening hours and arranging for their exam under the national open school system. This has worked very well and the credit goes to the DPC.

Convergence with horticulture and irrigation department is also satisfactory.

Payment is made within 14 days, although in many cases payment has been made within eight days.

Drawbacks

1. Job cards have not been updated in most of the villages.
2. The role of the GP is passive.

Annexure

S. No.	Name of member	Nomenclature	Names of districts visited
1.	K.B. Saxena	Chairman (Former Secretary, GoI)	Amravati, Dhalai, Dhamtari, Keonjhar, Narmada, Nicobar, Nizamabad, Pithoragarh, Sarguja, Salem, Thrissur and Vizianagaram
2.	Ashwini Kumar	Member	Amravati, Dhalai, Dhamtari, Sarguja, Keonjhar, Malkangiri, Narmada and Pithoragarh
3.	Rajendra Singh	Member	None
4.	Reetika Khera	Member	Allapuzha and Thrissur
5.	S.P. Singh	Member	Dhalai
6.	Hemnath Rao	Expert	Allapuzha, Coimbatore, Dhar, Khargaon, Nalanda, Nanded and Salem
7.	Nilay Ranjan	UNDP/MoRD	Allapuzha, Coimbatore, Dhamtari, Dhar, Khargaon, Nicobar and Pithoragarh
8.	V. Suresh Babu	Expert, NIRD	Coimbatore, Dhalai, Nalanda, Nanded, Nizamabad, Pithoragarh, Salem and Vizianagaram
9.	Pradip Prabhu	Expert	Dhalai and Nicobar
10.	G.N. Sharma	Expert (Civil Works)	Sarguja
11.	M.D. Asthana	Expert/Former Secretary, GoI	Allapuzha, Amravati, Coimbatore and Thrissur
12.	Bhagirath Panda	Expert, NEHU, Shillong	Allapuzha, Coimbatore, Keonjhar, Nizamabad, Salem and Vizianagaram
13.	Dayaram	Expert	Keonjhar
14.	K.S. Gopal	Expert	Malkangiri, Sarguja and Nanded
15.	Rajesh Mall	Researcher assisting Chairman, K.B. Saxena	Amravati, Dhalai, Dhamtari, Keonjhar, Narmada, Nizamabad, Pithoragarh, Sarguja, Salem, Thrissur and Vizianagaram

	State-wise listing of districts				Alphabetical listing of districts	
S. No.	State/Union Territory	District	Name of member/expert/ researcher visiting it	S. No.	District	State/Union Territory
1.	Andaman and Nicobar Islands	Nicobar	K.B. Saxena, Pradip Prabhu and Nilay Ranjan	1.	Allapuzha	Kerala
2.	Andhra Pradesh	Nizamabad	K.B. Saxena, V. Suresh Babu, Bhagirath Panda and Rajesh Mall	2.	Amravati	Maharashtra
	Andhra Pradesh	Vizianagaram	K.B. Saxena, V. Suresh Babu, Bhagirath Panda and Rajesh Mall	3.	Coimbatore	Tamil Nadu
3.	Bihar	Nalanda	Hemnath Rao and V. Suresh Babu	4.	Dhalai	Tripura
4.	Chhattisgarh	Dhamtari	K.B. Saxena, Ashwini Kumar, Nilay Ranjan and Rajesh Mall	5.	Dhamtari	Chhattisgarh
	Chhattisgarh	Sarguja	K.B. Saxena, Ashwini Kumar, K.S. Gopal, G.N. Sharma and Rajesh Mall	6.	Dhar	Madhya Pradesh

(Continued)

(Continued)

	State-wise listing of districts				Alphabetical listing of districts	
S. No.	State/Union Territory	District	Name of member/expert/ researcher visiting it	S. No.	District	State/Union Territory
5.	Gujarat	Narmada	K.B. Saxena, Ashwini Kumar, K.S. Gopal and Rajesh Mall	7.	Keonjhar	Odisha
6.	Kerala	Allapuzha	Hemnath Rao, Nilay Ranjan, Bhagirath Panda and Reetika Khera	8.	Khargaon	Madhya Pradesh
	Kerala	Thrissur	K.B. Saxena, V. Suresh Babu, M.D. Asthana, Reetika Khera and Rajesh Mall	9.	Malkangiri	Odisha
7.	Madhya Pradesh	Dhar	Hemnath Rao and Nilay Ranjan	10.	Nalanda	Bihar
	Madhya Pradesh	Khargaon	Hemnath Rao and Nilay Ranjan	11.	Nanded	Maharashtra
8.	Maharashtra	Amravati	K.B. Saxena, Dayaram, Ashwini Kumar, M.D. Asthana and Rajesh Mall	12.	Narmada	Gujarat
	Maharashtra	Nanded	Hemnath Rao and V. Suresh Babu	13.	Nicobar	Andaman and Nicobar Islands
9.	Odisha	Keonjhar	K.B. Saxena, Ashwini Kumar, Bhagirath Panda and Rajesh Mall	14.	Nizamabad	Andhra Pradesh
	Odisha	Malkangiri	K.S. Gopal and Ashwini Kumar	15.	Pithoragarh	Uttarakhand
10.	Tamil Nadu	Coimbatore	V. Suresh Babu, Nilay Ranjan, Bhagirath Panda, Hemnath Rao and M.D. Asthana	16.	Salem	Tamil Nadu
	Tamil Nadu	Salem	K.B. Saxena, V. Suresh Babu, Hemnath Rao, Bhagirath Panda and Rajesh Mall	17.	Sarguja	Chhattisgarh
11.	Tripura	Dhalai	K.B. Saxena, V. Suresh Babu, Pradip Prabhu, Ashwini Kumar, S.P. Singh and Rajesh Mall	18.	Thrissur	Kerala
12.	Uttarakhand	Pithoragarh	K.B. Saxena, V. Suresh Babu, Nilay Ranjan and Rajesh Mall	19.	Vizianagaram	Andhra Pradesh

ANNEXURE 3
District-wise report/summary observations submitted by members/experts

S. No.	District	State/Union Territory	Name of member/expert	Page nos.
1.	Allapuzha	Kerala	Hemnath Rao, Nilay Ranjan, Bhagirath Panda and Reetika Khera	39
2.	Amravati	Maharashtra	Dayaram and M.D. Asthana	42
3.	Coimbatore	Tami Nadu	V. Suresh Babu, Nilay Ranjan, Bhagirath Panda, Hemnath Rao and M.D. Asthana	44
4.	Dhalai	Tripura	V. Suresh Babu and Pradip Prabhu	47
5.	Dhamtari	Chhattisgarh	See K.B. Saxena's comments in main report	53
6.	Dhar	Madhya Pradesh	Hemnath Rao with Nilay Ranjan	54
7.	Keonjhar	Odisha	Bhagirath Panda	55
8.	Khargaon	Madhya Pradesh	Hemnath Rao with Nilay Ranjan	56
9.	Malkangiri	Odisha	K.S. Gopal	58
10.	Nalanda	Bihar	Hemnath Rao and V. Suresh Babu	59
11.	Nanded	Maharashtra	Hemnath Rao and V. Suresh Babu	61
12.	Narmada	Gujarat	K.S. Gopal	63
13.	Nicobar	Andaman and Nicobar Islands	K.B. Saxena, Pradip Prabhu and Nilay Ranjan	64

(Continued)

(Continued)

S. No.	District	State/Union Territory	Name of member/expert	Page nos.
14.	Nizamabad	Andhra Pradesh	V. Suresh Babu and Bhagirath Panda	66
15.	Pithoragarh	Uttarakhand	K.B. Saxena (with writing inputs of Rajesh Mall), V. Suresh Babu and Ashwini Kumar	69
16.	Salem	Tamil Nadu	V. Suresh Babu, Hemnath Rao and Bhagirath Panda	80
17.	Sarguja	Chhattisgarh	K.S. Gopal and G.N. Sharma	83
18.	Thrissur	Kerala	K.B. Saxena (with writing inputs of Rajesh Mall), V. Suresh Babu, Reetika Khera and M.D. Asthana	84
19.	Vizianagaram	Andhra Pradesh	V. Suresh Babu and Bhagirath Panda	88

Index